The Sewing Connection Series V

Many thanks to: David Larson Productions
5910 North Lilly Road
Menomonee Falls, Wisconsin 53051

Dave and Kate, producers
Director Ivy Lyn Revolinski and Jeff Cartier,
David C. Larson, Jim Lillis, Peter Pfankuch,
Tom Reardon, Mary Reidinger, Andy Steiber.
Models Kristina Larson and Kathy Thompson.
Photographers Marty Savasta, Wilbur Tague

Special thanks to: Viking Sewing Machine Company
11750 Berea Road
Cleveland, Ohio 44111

My undying gratitude to my dear friend, Rebecca Feehan Adams, who knows everything about computers ... so I don't have to.

Copyright © 1992
Shirley Adams Publications • 922 Cheltenham Way • Plainfield, IN 46168

All rights reserved. No part of this book may be reproduced in any form or by any means without the prior written consent of the author.

Printed in the United States of America

The Sewing Connection Series V

1. ***Setting Boundaries:***
   Bordering collars or clothing edges provides a pleasant frame 1

2. ***Sueded Silk and Microfibers:***
   Beautifully textured fabrics require special consideration 6

3. ***Shawl Collars:***
   A simple conversion can change a standard collar 11

4. ***Testing ... 1 2 3:***
   Whys and Hows of making test patterns before cutting into expensive fabric ... 16

5. ***Embellishing The Truth:***
   Acquired some ugly fabric? Improvements may be possible 20

6. ***Love To Sew With My Feet:***
   Jan Saunders guests demonstrating clever uses of presser feet 23

7. ***Terrific Tubes:***
   Making fabric tubes and using them in clothing or accessories 28

8. ***See It, Sew It:***
   Adapting features from ready-to-wear using commercial patterns 33

9. ***See It Again, New Flavor:***
   Many ideas in ready-to-wear that another segment demonstrates 38

10. ***Home Dec Camouflage:***
    Covering a folding screen, shoulders of garments in a closet, a lamp shade 41

11. ***Wearing Home Dec Fabrics:***
    Whether the fashions are big or little, home dec fabric has much to offer 45

12. ***A Baker's Dozen:***
    A multitude of sewing tips in a mixed bag 50

13. ***It's In The Bag:***
    With any type fabric, bags give opportunity for self expression 55

Program 1: Setting Boundaries

Welcome back to Series V of *The Sewing Connection* ... your connection to the world of fashion because anything you see you can make if you sew. A major delight is falling for a designer ensemble of enormous cost and knowing you can duplicate it on your terms at a fraction of the cost. Sometimes it is even possible to find identical fabric which really makes you chuckle ... while you marvel at your wisdom in learning to sew. Is any other hobby as satisfyingly productive?

The suit and blouse on the cover are examples of garments which are designer adaptations using standard patterns with a few simple changes. The pattern for the blouse collar and front in the center of this book is to be added to a tailored shirt type blouse pattern of your own.

The jacket is a pattern I've used many times before, this time with the addition of a border of contrasting fabric around all edges to set a boundary. This pattern has a semi-fit at the waistline for a little figure flattery. The shaping is produced by vertical darts in the front and back pattern pieces and shaped side seams. The pattern is very simple with only a back, front, sleeve major pieces plus the front and back facings. Such a pattern is found in every brand and is very appropriate for the other boundary ... the matching of plaids which also sets some limitations.

When choosing such a pattern, look carefully at the line drawing in the pattern book or on the envelope. If the bust dart is horizontal, the pattern is unusable for plaids. The reason for this is that a sleeve should blend in completely with the jacket body with a continuation of horizontal stripes

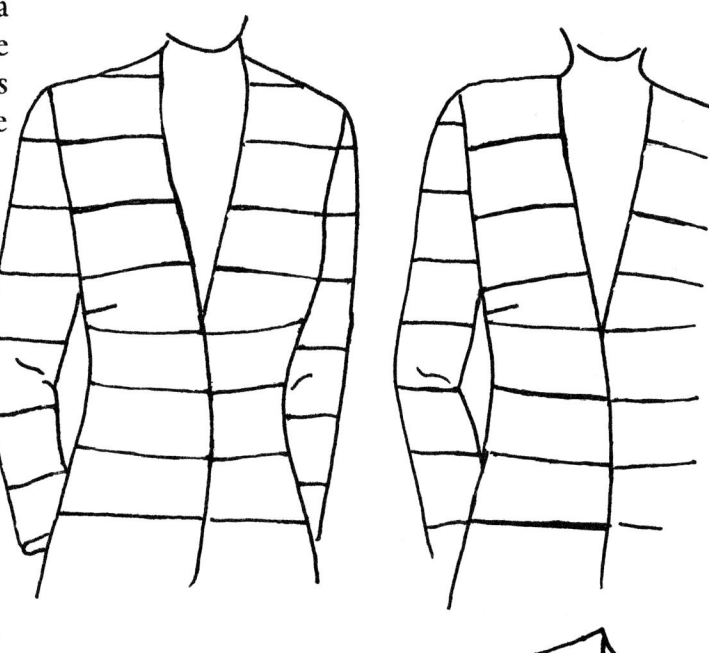

all up and down coinciding. A dart would break this up so that matching is possible above or below, but not both places. This, as illustrated, is unacceptable.

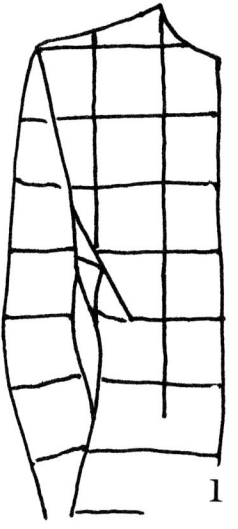

A diagonal dart is equally unacceptable as it distorts the plaid unreasonably when the two dart lines are stitched together.

Vertical darts work because the horizontal stripes stay in position. The vertical stripes of the fabric must be watched, however, as to make this match as attractively as possible the dart should be centered on a group of lines. This illustration shows the perfect chevrons which result with proper positioning.

This dart positioning is sometimes done when the pattern is being placed on the fabric. Sometimes it is moving the dart slightly to the left or right, after cutting out, when marking and stitching. To be thus moved slightly doesn't appreciably effect the fit. The slight sacrifice is well worth it when one considers the finished appearance. Tuck this information away until you need to apply it later.

The starting point, however, is laying the pattern pieces on the plaid, **front piece** first, as that is the most important or the most noticeable piece. You may double the fabric to cut both layers at once, but only if all the plaid lines exactly coincide between the two layers. It is usually easier to cut one layer of each piece doing all the thinking and matching on it. Then turn over these cut pieces until they blend into the uncut plaid lines and cut all the left pieces without having to think. Watch the horizontal lines to avoid emphasizing with bright stripes any body locations better left concealed. The center front is usually centered on a vertical stripe group. This illustration shows a layout that works for all main pieces.

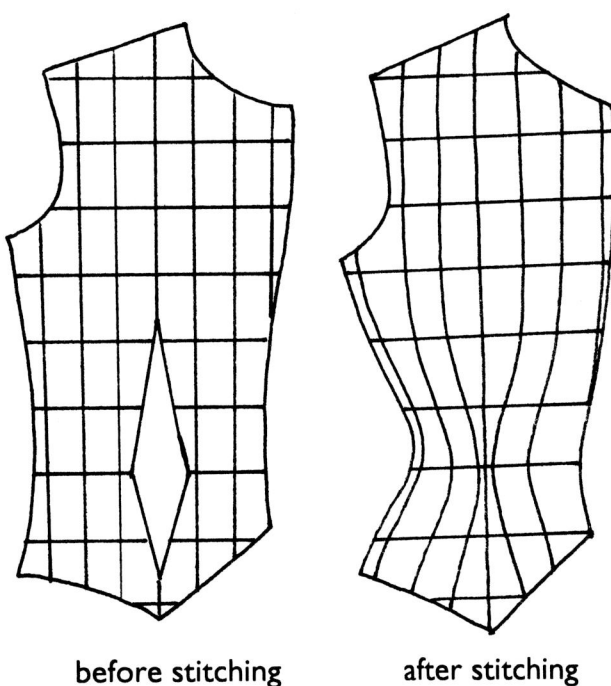

before stitching   after stitching

or in a skirt

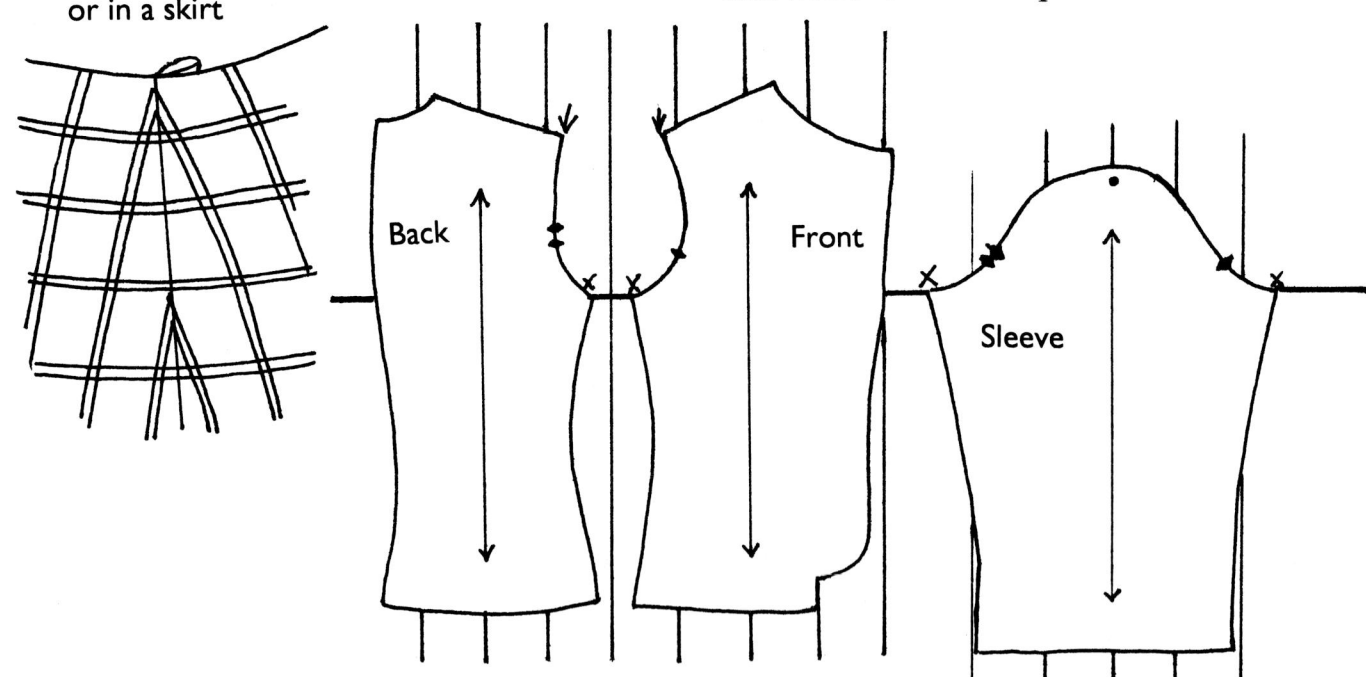

Notice the underarm **X** at the side seam of the jacket front. Place the point which will stitch to it (the side seam of the back) at the same horizontal stripe in a mirror image position in relation to the vertical stripe next to it. This insures a perfect chevroning of the stripes when the seam is stitched.

Now look at the shoulder edge points and be sure these are at the same vertical position. A matching stripe front and back going across the shoulder seam is what this produces.

The sleeve will always be a perfect match if the underarm point is lined up on the same horizontal as those points of pattern front and back. FORGET matching the armscye notches as every article tells you to do because it probably will not, in most cases, produce a match. Because of the different shape and slant of the sleeve cap compared to the garment armscye, matching at a notch does nothing to line up stripes throughout the whole sleeve length. There are too many exceptions such as dropped shoulder seams or extended shoulders or raglan cuts curving up into the neck. Matching a notch would not work for any of these. The underarm point match-up always works. Probably a vertical match (sleeve to jacket) is unlikely, again because of different shapes, so perhaps just center a prominent vertical stripe down the sleeve middle will be best.

For the solid border, I took a cue from a horrendously expensive designer suit and noticed that no top stitching showed. This indicates that not just a later addition, the border was rather a displacement for part of the plaid edge. This involves a careful planning to determine what must be done first, what next, etc. These steps produce the desired results:

1. Cut out the jacket front.
2. Using the same pattern, cut out a 2" wide contrast fabric strip for the front neck, down the front, then over across the bottom to the side seam.
3. Cut out a fusible interfacing, using the same pattern front, for the entire front. Because jackets like this are usually loosely woven wools of bouclé yarns, a fusible interfacing is especially valuable to hold everything firmly together. In addition, it provides the necessary body and understructure for a well-tailored suit.
4. Cut 1 3/8" off interfacing in locations where trim will be on the edge. Fuse the cut off piece to the back side of contrast trim. Fuse the major remaining piece to the jacket inside.
5. At any inside corners the trim will have, reinforce with tiny stitches within the seam allowance, making a **V** as illustrated. Then slash to the point of that **V**.

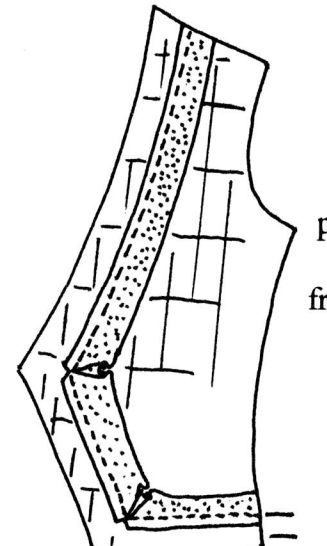

6. Right sides together, pin the inside edge of the trim to the outer jacket front edge. The trim edge should be 7/8" in from the outer jacket edge. You

} 5/8" seam
} 7/8"

3

would be stitching 1 3/8" from the jacket edge as you stitch the 5/8" seam on the trim.

7. Press this seam open, clipping any curved area where it pulls. Trim both seam allowances off short, down to about 3/8". Get a good flat press using steam and the pressure of a press or an iron, or aided by the use of a clapper if necessary. It is now treated as one piece of fabric and is the same size as the original front because the trim has displaced the original edge.

Handle the back piece, lower edge and neck, the same way before jacket back and front are joined. Or join seams first, apply trim after.

Later the facing will be stitched to the lining edge, then the facing-lining unit can simply be stitched all around to the jacket edge, right sides together. Press open, grade the seam allowances (trim them off two different widths to flatten as much as possible), turn right side out and press the outer edge flat.

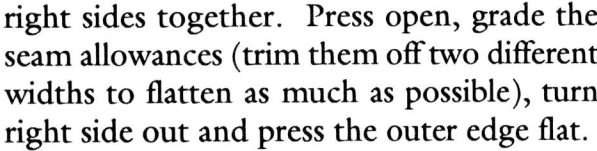

On the sleeves, a trim was added as a faux vent. That vent projection simply had the seam allowance pressed under and the outer fold was stitched down by hand.

When hemming linings, be sure to leave about 1/2" or so of lengthwise ease, both in the body of the jacket as well as in the sleeves. This is to prevent horizontal folds of fabric in the outside of the jacket caused by a short lining which pulls it up. The how-to of the process is explained in *The Sewing Connection* Book II for those who desire further instruction.

This border around neck and front edges, sleeve hems, so popular now, can also be done by using an exterior facing as is often seen on blouses or dresses. This is done by first interfacing the facing with a sheer fusible. The facing is a contrasting color or texture or print if it is to later show up as a definite border. Pin the RIGHT side of the facing to the WRONG side of the garment edge and stitch the outer 5/8" seam. Press open if possible (depending on curved or straight line), or if not, simply grade the seam two different widths to stagger the bulk and eliminate an outer ridge. If unable to press open the seam before grading, it will be necessary to hand baste this edge flat after turning the facing to the outside for the greatest accuracy in pressing flat.

Also consider the inner edge. This may be pressed under a seam's width either before or after the outer edge is handled. If there are any square corners, a reinforcement V stitching may be wise to prevent any fraying when that inside corner is clipped.

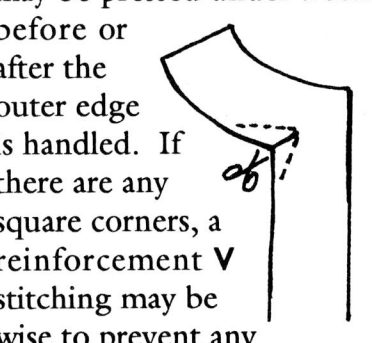

If buttonholes will be made in this band, they must be vertical so that the button stays centered. If horizontal, the buttons would slide to the edge ... off center.

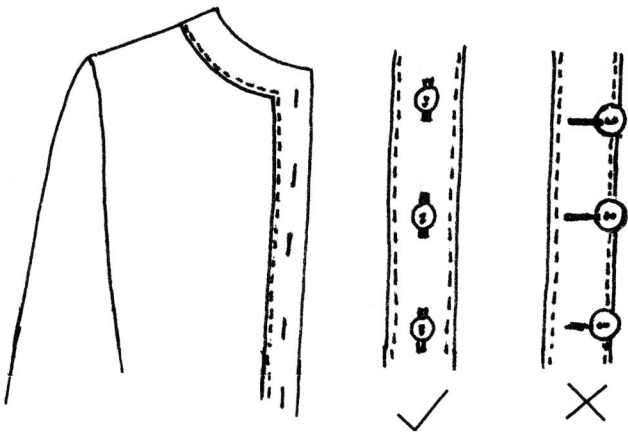

Grosgrain ribbon, about 3/4" or so wide is currently being used as a border at wrists, collar, lapels. Choose one of the softer, nicer varieties if using. It is likely this ribbon will shrink when pressed, so it would be wise to steam press it before applying. At the same time you press it, shape it into a slight curve IF that would conform with lapel shape. Machine topstitching the edges is one alternative, but for a softer application, hand stitching may be preferable. This would also make for easier removal should the borders slip out of fashion in the future and you wish to restore the suit to its original condition. Temporarily the border will update an existing suit, giving it a new lease on life.

Many other border suggestions can be found in Book III of *The Sewing Connection*.

Program 2: Sueded Silks and Microfibers

Fabrics in these categories are so lovely, to touch them is tranquilizing. To wear them is therapeutic. Sheer, soft luxury both, they are marvelous for so many articles of clothing requiring soft, drapey fabric hand.

The silks have been around since antiquity. Little silk worms still spin these beautiful fibers. The new twist here is the surface ... sand washed, sueded texture. A slightly frosty look accompanies the wonderful velvety tactile quality because in the finishing process a little color rubs off. This is perfectly acceptable and part of the prestige look.

The microfibers in a **woven** fabrication are pretty new. Microfibers have actually been around for about twenty years extruded in a solid sheet we know as UltraSuede®. It's only recently that manufacturers are taking these micro denier polyester fibers, which means they are finer than spider web, and twisting them into yarns for weaving into fabrics. You may be able to tell the difference between silks and microfibers by looking and feeling. Then again, you may have to check the labels or hang tags to be sure of which is which.

The differences between the silks and microfibers will definitely include price, as the silks will be more expensive. The care of silk may be more involved than the microfibers, but not necessarily. Many treat them the same. There may be a little progressive color loss for the silks depending on your treatment, and especially in spot removal which must be done with care to prevent rubbing out color. On the other hand, all polyesters have an affinity for oils so may pick up oily soil more easily, but will release it without color loss. The comfort, the luxurious feel, the breathability of natural fibers is found in both. Both are beautifully packable and therefore, great travelers.

Those on the market are aimed at a variety of end uses. The very light weight silks and microfibers will be used for blouses or dresses of course, an obvious use. Choose patterns with soft styling, asymmetrical drapes, gathers. The blouse I am wearing on the book cover is sand-washed silk which can be smashed flat in a suitcase and when removed, never show a crease. The cascade ruffle at the buttoned closing is actually a shawl collar explained in program 3 and the pattern for it is the book centerfold. The oversized green blouse on the colored photo pages is also a sueded silk, Infatuation® by Logantex. It has no drapes or gathers, but its man-tailored enormous amount of ease hangs beautifully on a body, showing its soft drapey quality. The purple dress in the same photo is UltraSuedes's Silkmore®. The look and feel are similar, but it is a synthetic polyester microfiber. This dress has also been a frequent traveler and quite carefree.

Recently these same blouse or dress weight silks and microfibers have been seen made up as blazer-type jackets, lined or unlined, by many manufacturers. This thin fabric used in tailored styles is contrary to traditional usage, but works well with two additions. The framework or superstructure of shoulder pads from which it hangs holds it in place beautifully. When fashion eliminates pads, this unconventional combination might not be a good idea. The second reason it is possible is that a fusible interfacing both beefs up the front and gives support to construction details such as pockets. Examining ready-to-wear would probably reveal a thin fusible interfacing (such as will be suggested later in this program) on the entire jacket front and undercollar. A second layer of the thin interfacing might then be fused to the upper-collar-facing unit for a little more firmness in a necessary area.

Interfacing used over large areas in this manner is utilitarian and not meant to be seen. It would be a good idea to cover it with a pretty lining. Unlined jackets should only have abbreviated interfacings where they do not show, such as in facings and collars.

Some heavier fabrications of microfibers do very well for sportswear and separates. They are also soft and drapey to produce cowl necklines, gathers, side draping. Their additional weight makes them also desirable for pants and skirts, anoraks or other types of jackets. Again, their soft downy surface is pleasant and luxurious. Examples of these are UltraSuedes's Sherice® and Logantex Charisma®.

Rainwear is another possibility from the microfibers and seen in ready-to-wear as well as over-the-counter yardage. Vanessa® from UltraSuede is a satiny, taffeta-like water-repellent fabric with colors to boost the spirits as well as keeping one dry on dreary days. La Ultima® from Logantex has a Zepel finish to trap out the rain, and is a little heavier with a softer hand.

With any of the sand-washed silks and microfibers, having chosen the styling and pattern it will be paired with is accomplishing a large part of the challenge. The next consideration is care treatment after the garment is made and therefore, what pre-treatment before cutting out will be necessary.

To begin with the sand-washed silks, a wide variety of recommendations comes from varied sources. Frequently the bolt says dry clean only. This absolves the manufacturer from blame should you choose to wash it and the results are undesirable. Purchased blouses may also say dry clean only and, if this is a fitted garment, I may choose to dry clean it. Also, however, with a fitted garment the understructure is probably such that dry cleaning would be better. If this is a blouse and by its very nature oversize and blouesy, you may prefer to wash it, risking the possibility of a little shrinkage which would probably not matter. If it is white I would especially want to wash it, as so frequently it would return from the cleaners with a hint of some pastel color.

Let's return to yardage and consider alternatives before cutting. The gentlest wash would be by hand with a very mild soap solution such as a liquid dish wash or even baby shampoo in cold water. Some also advocate vinegar to set the color. Other studies completely dismiss the vinegar theory as being of no validity. The wet fabric could then be rolled in a towel after rinsing to remove excess moisture before pressing while damp, on the wrong side.

An intermediate technique is machine washing on a delicate cycle with a mild liquid soap, warm or cold water, line drying before pressing.

The sand-washed silks on this program were all done in my washer with no special treatment. They were put in a regular wash load of dark-colored clothes, warm water, and regular laundry detergent. Cold rinse water was used. Rough fabrics such as some denim jeans might even have been in that load. I have in fact, washed some blouse silk yardage on various occasions with rough fabrics to purposely create a sand-washed effect when none was originally there.

Typical of these sueded silks is not only the sueded surface, but also a slight irregularity of color here and there is not objectionable. Look at the ready-to-wear to reaffirm this. To dry I put the yardage in the dryer with only a few other items on a gentle cycle, reserving part of that wash load for later drying. When the silk was dry I took it immediately from the dryer and hung it over a railing for a little while. Pressing the wrong side with a steam iron took only a slight touch up. To pretreat it thus means that the same treatment may later be used each time on the garment. You must make your own decision on how you will care for this beautiful fabric and don't blame me if you ruin it!

Any of the microfibers do just fine with machine wash, then dryer or line dry as you choose. Either way, don't press creases in as you would on the sleeves of a man's cotton dress shirt. To press silky sleeves in the round without creases give a more elegant look, and a dryer might help achieve that goal by having the fabric mainly fluffed out before the pressing begins.

When laying the pattern or when sewing, use fine pins to prevent holes showing later. If the pin is as large as .55 millimeters, it is probably too large. .5 pins do quite well and once used, anything heavier seems like using nails! Be careful that a damaged pin doesn't pull a yarn in the fabric.

Fusible or sew-in interfacings, suitably sheer, can both be used successfully. With a fusible interfacing it is a little exasperating to cut that small piece, then cut the small slippery facing and get the two to mesh perfectly while fusing. It is easier to cut the interfacing, fuse it to the uncut fabric of the facing, then cut around it to perfectly cut the facing in its true shape. With the light weight silks and microfibers, my current favorites are HTC's Sew Sheer®, Sof Brush® or Touch of Gold®. The later two can be fused with a lower temperature so are especially good for the microfibers. New products come out frequently so do keep trying any new ones which might be the perfect choice for you. In the slightly heavier weights, an old tried and true product, HTC Fusi-Knit® works well. Here also however, several other possibilities exist, so explore the market to compare qualities to find your favorite.

To sew, use the smallest needle. #60/8, #65/9 or a maximum of #70/10 in a sharp needle (change to a new one frequently) can be used. The smaller, the better to prevent puckering. You might also try the smallest denim needle (probably a #70/10) which works well because of its extreme sharpness. Make the stitches small to also prevent a puckered look, about 15 per inch. Consider also (if you will be straight stitching only), using a straight stitch foot and a straight stitch throat plate. These allow less play in the fabric and that also prevents puckering. Moving the needle position might also be helpful in preventing a fabric play or bounce. I usually tend toward a little taut sewing ... holding the fabric firmly in front and back of the stitching point. **DO NOT** pull or force the fabric as this could throw off your machine timing.

Many advocate a particular brand of thread, the reasoning being that some brands stretch and shrink, again causing puckering. Others say less puckering occurs if the fabric is cut on the crosswise grain instead of lengthwise. To test these two factors I stitched a trial sample of two layers of fabric. 8 different thread brands and kinds (cotton, poly, silk, etc.) were tested in **L** shaped rows to see the effect of grain direction. They all looked exactly the same, concluding that thread brand and stitching direction made no difference in this case. If stitching together an interfaced piece to a single layer, however, stitch with the more stable interfaced layer on top to prevent scooting.

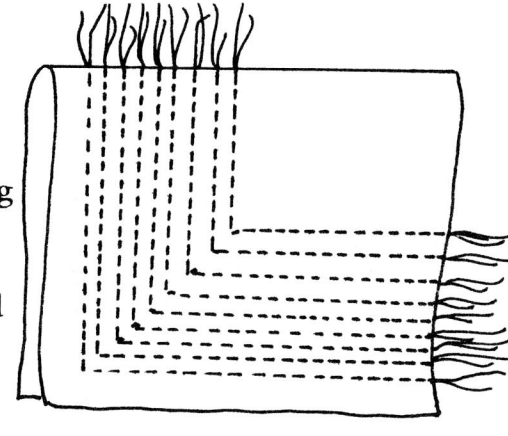

Buttonholes on interfaced silkies present no problems. Hems are also easy on most of these and especially if it is a print fabric, rendering hem invisible. Unfortunately, on some very sensitive solid colors the hems may show up more than you want. Make a decision by trying techniques on leftover scraps. If a serged edge shows an impression on the outside when pressed, try a hem tape or lace to see if this is flatter. Another possibility, if fraying is not a problem, is to pink the hem edge and catch stitch **between** layers, not over the edge.

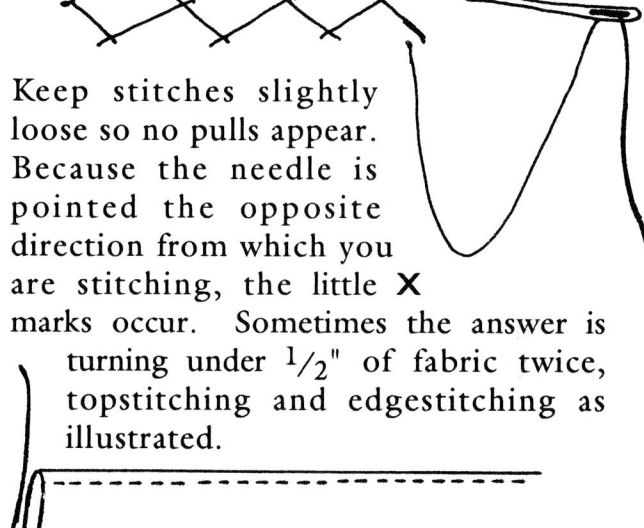

Keep stitches slightly loose so no pulls appear. Because the needle is pointed the opposite direction from which you are stitching, the little **X** marks occur. Sometimes the answer is turning under $1/2$" of fabric twice, topstitching and edgestitching as illustrated.

These solid color delicates might also be a good place to use a skirt underlining for two reasons. A very thin silk or microfiber could stand some "beefing up" making it heavier. The other reason is that a hem which shows looks tacky, but hemming to the underlining rather than to itself makes it invisible, elegant. To refresh your memory about the difference between lining and underlining ...

Lining is a skirt constructed separately from the outside skirt fabric, but probably cut from the same pattern. The two layers are then connected at the waistline and around the zipper, but hemmed separately.

Underlining is cut from the same pattern and each piece is staystitched at top and sides to the fashion fabric before seams are constructed. This is sometimes called

piece lining. When the hem is turned up, it is carefully hemmed by hand to the underlining, being very careful not to catch through to the outside fashion fabric. This avoids the "dimples" a caught stitch would cause and elevates the garment value.

Lovely fabrics, both of these. You'll enjoy living with them and be glad you decided to buy them to include in your wardrobe.

Special thanks to:

Handler Textile Corp.
450 Seventh Avenue
New York, NY 10123

Logantex®, Incorporated
1460 Broadway
New York, NY 10036

UltraSuede® Fabrics
104 West 40 Street
New York, NY 10018

TIP: The very fine straight pins and denim needles mentioned can be found, if not sold locally, in notions catalog: Clotilde's
1909 SW First Avenue
Ft. Lauderdale, FL 33315

Program 3: *Shawl Collars*

A shawl collar is an interesting feature you can add to a garment. Its distinguishing marks are a center back seam and the rearrangement of units. This means that the collar is no longer a separate piece. The undercollar becomes one with the garment front. The upper collar and front facing are likewise joined together in another unit. The way this is accomplished is miraculously easy, despite instructions to the contrary seen in most flat pattern books.

The garments on which this change is possible are endless. A shawl collar is equally appropriate on a blouse, a dress, a suit, a coat. The basic method for making this combination follows.

Here is a pattern for a basic full roll collar, half size so it easily fits on the paper. The collar pattern you find in any of the commercial patterns is very similar.

dot to the center back measures the same as your bodice back. The distance in front of the shoulder dot is always longer than the distance in back of it because that's how your body is ... front neckline lower than back.

This collar would typically be worn folded down in back, that fold called the breakline. Inward from the fold is the stand, outward from it is the fall. The two are of equal height. If the neckline is worn buttoned up, the break would extend to the center front as the dotted line on the right illustrates. If worn as an open, unbuttoned neckline, the breakline would fold short of the center front as the left side shows.

The outer style line is whatever you, the designer, make it. Fashion decrees this line sometimes big and wide with long

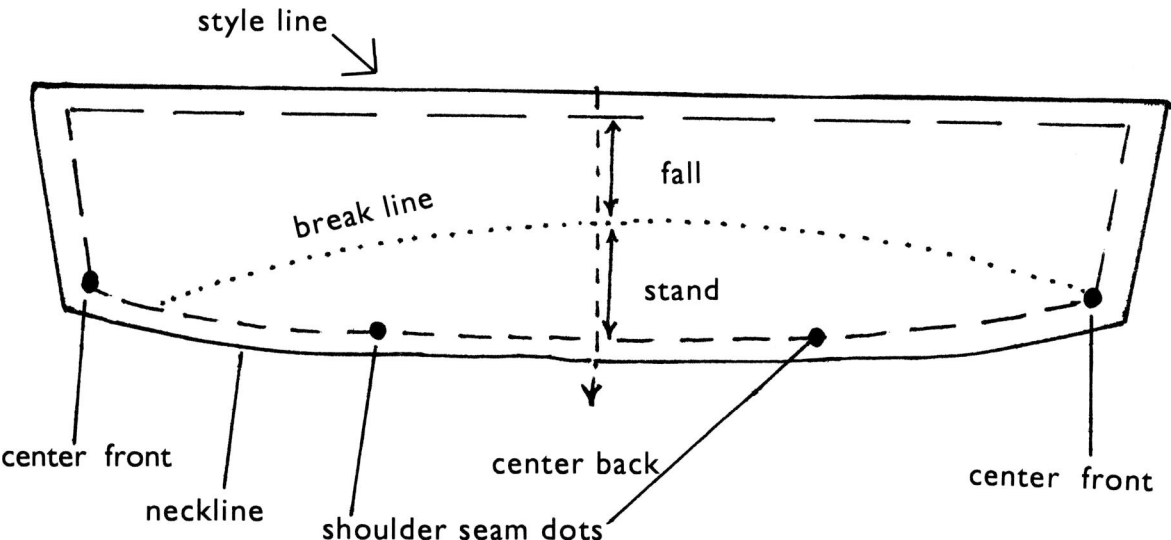

The neckline always measures exactly the same as the bodice neckline to which it will be stitched **at the stitching line**, not at the outside cutting line. From the center front dot to the shoulder seam dot fits the bodice front neckline. From that shoulder

points. At other times, it is small with squared front points. It stitches to nothing but itself so there are no restrictions on it.

If your commercial pattern is a coat or suit, there will be two pattern pieces.

The upper collar will be larger allowing for the turn of the cloth, as heavier fabric would be used. The smaller undercollar pattern would usually be only 1/2 a collar to be cut double layers. A center back seam would be added, and a bias direction grain arrow for a more fluid folding when interfaced. If the pattern is for a dress or blouse (anticipating thin fabric) there is usually only one pattern piece to be cut double layers and both the same size.

Now that you know more about a basic collar than you probably ever cared to know, we can proceed!

Fold your collar pattern in half at the center back. Place its shoulder dot exactly on the bodice pattern corner where the shoulder and neck stitching lines converge (refer to figure above).

With a pin pushed in to hold the two patterns in place, use that as a pivot point and revolve the collar front around until the center front dot exactly coincides with the line on your bodice pattern marked center front (refer to figure below).

That's all! You have made a shawl collar that easily! If you place an L square (a sheet of paper will do to find a 90° angle) on the shoulder, you will notice that the angle formed by the collar - shoulder is slightly smaller than 90° (refer to figure below).

Pin the two pattern pieces together and use them as a combined unit to cut out the bodice front - undercollar fabric.

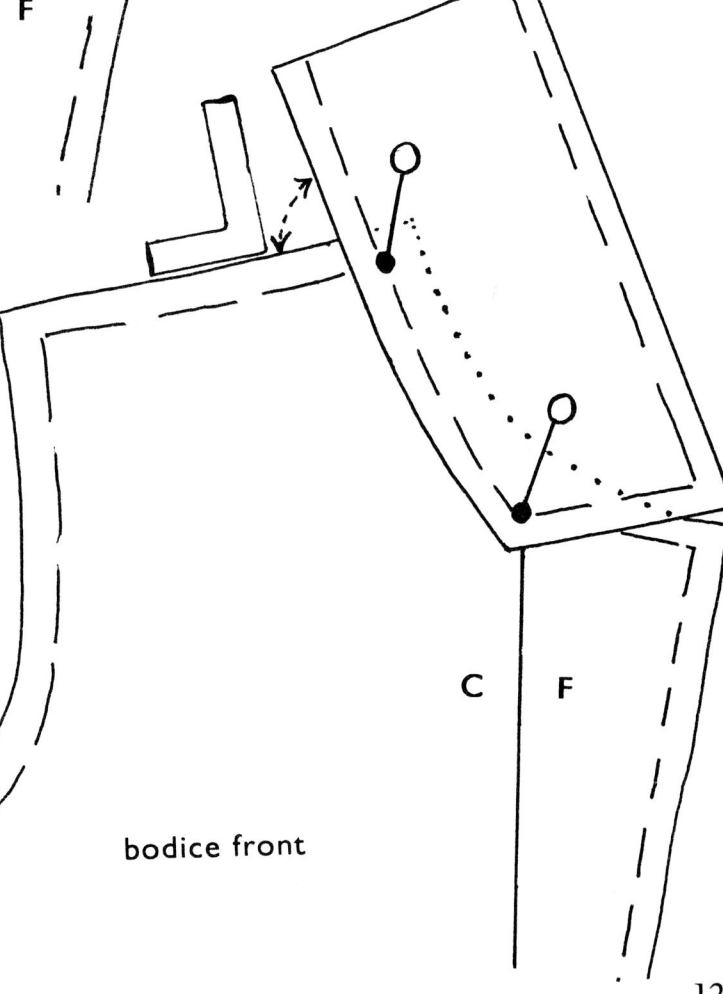

12

When cutting **be sure to add a center back seam** allowance as shown here.

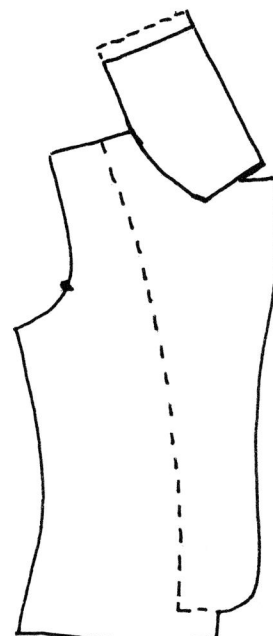

For the upper collar-facing unit, use the very same pattern, but only the center front part from the dotted line, omitting the side bodice. If this is heavy fabric, remember to add a little extra as previously described around collar style line. For thin blouse or dress fabric, cut no extra.

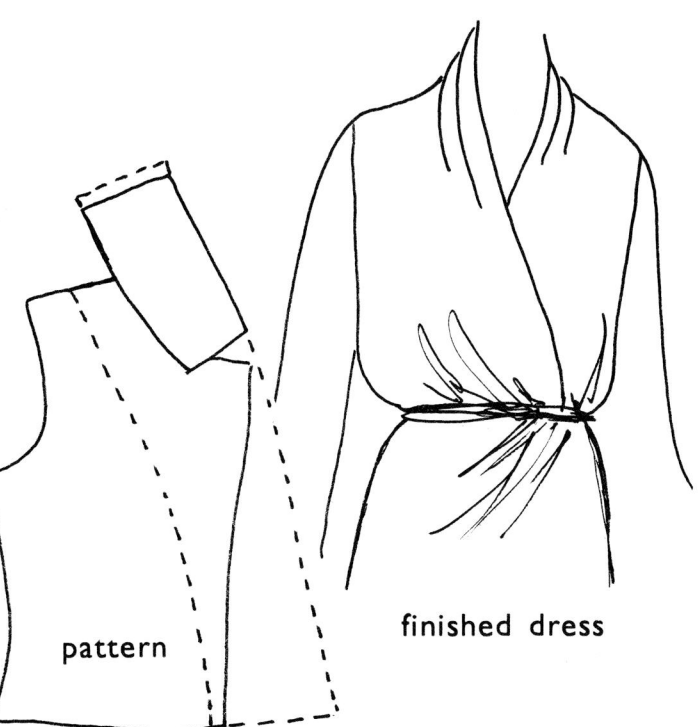

pattern

finished dress

print dress is a stand up collar, its height shortened by stitching two pleats around the neck back as the finished dress above shows.

The above pattern dotted line shows that the only actual change from the original is to cut a front line diagonally out wider to the bottom to produce the lapover or surplice closing. The interior dotted line just shows that the facing layer would be cut the usual way.

The purple dress below has been cut

The bodice back will remain unchanged. The collar back should exactly fit it, but you will encounter that inside-outside corner stitching area at each neck-shoulder corner when constructing the garment. Refer back to program 1 of this book for directions on how to stitch the two together perfectly. If you want a back facing and your pattern didn't include one, merely use the bodice back pattern, cutting the neck section only. The shoulder width of this facing should measure the same as the front facing width.

You're designing now. Remember you have the freedom to change that outer style line any way you choose. The program 3 photos in the middle of the book illustrate some possibilities. The

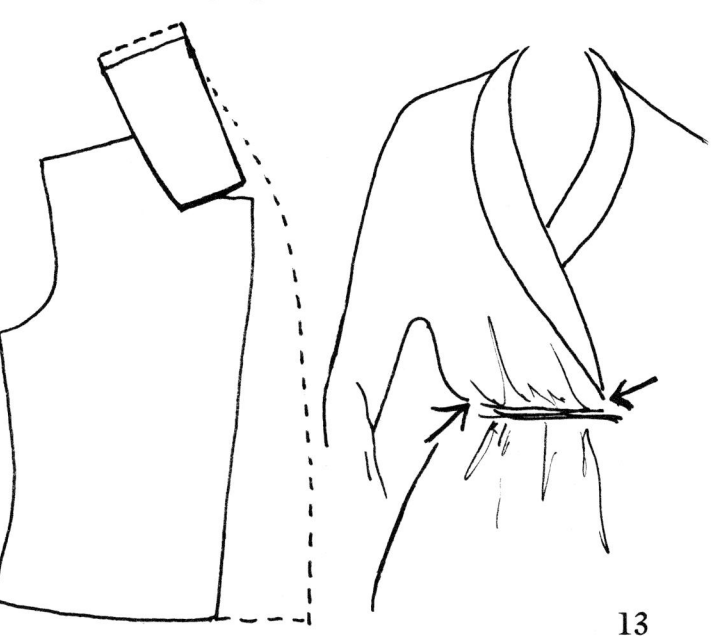

almost identically, with just slightly more curve in the collar style line. Also, the back collar pleats were left out so it folds over as collars usually do. No buttons--hooks and eyes fasten the waist in two places (arrows, bottom page 13) to keep the double breasted width in place.

On the cover of *The Sewing Connection Series* **IV** book was featured a fur collar on an UltraLeather® suit, reprinted in this book center photos. That shawl collar, illustrated on the right, was made by this same technique, but it was removeable, buttoning to the inside of the coat. The upper collar was all the manmade fur. The undercollar and both layers of the back facing were cut in the leather for less bulk. Notice the shape of this detachable collar.

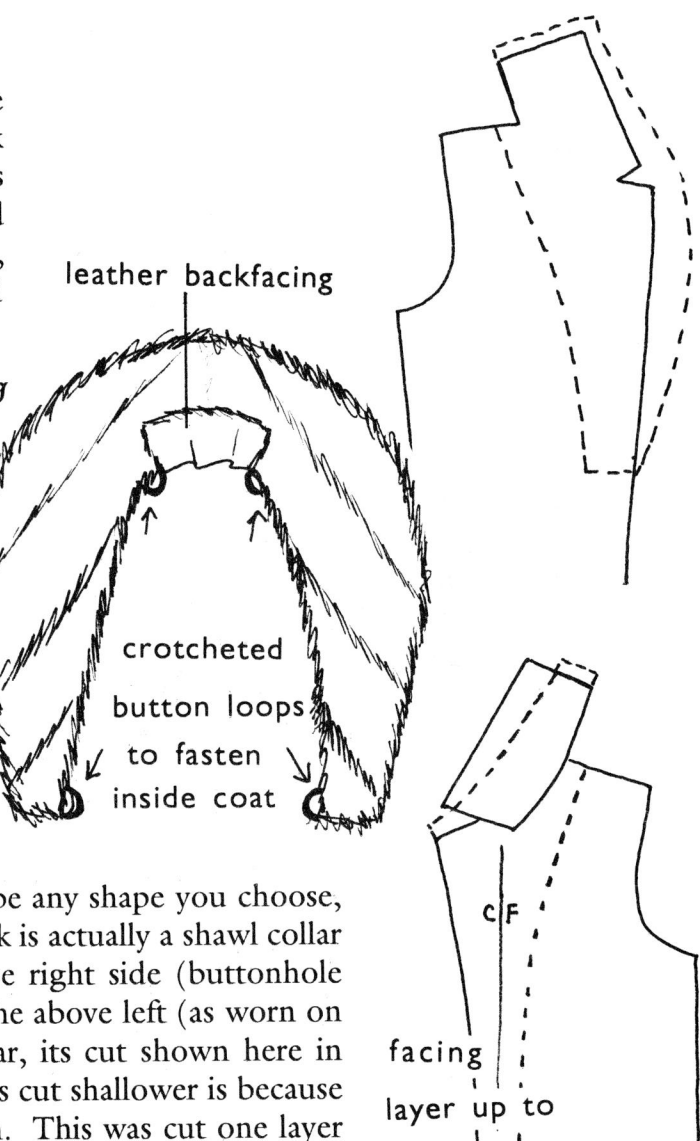

Remembering that outer style line can be any shape you choose, the blue-purple blouse on the cover of this book is actually a shawl collar also! Great liberties were taken on the blouse right side (buttonhole side) to produce the cascade ruffle closing. The above left (as worn on the body) is just a simple, pointed shawl collar, its cut shown here in these dotted lines. The reason the collar back is cut shallower is because it is not folded over, but stands up when worn. This was cut one layer for the blouse and one layer for the facing with also a layer of suitably sheer interfacing. This will later have the buttons sewn on.

To make the right front and its facing is the tricky part. What produces the cascade ruffle is that the right collar area is considerably larger than the left side. There is more space between each buttonhole than between the corresponding buttons, thus the flounce in each little space. This figure on the left shows how the pattern was traced on another piece of paper or better yet, the fibrous pattern tracer purchased in interfacing departments of fabric shops. The dotted lines show where slashes were made with scissors in **A**. Figure **B** shows how the pattern looks when all the slashed areas are opened up, each an equal amount out at the style line. It is carefully mounted on a second piece of paper to back the slashed area. Trim off excess paper and you have the right side of your blouse, dotted line indicating the interfacing and facing single layers.

Notice what has happened in the asterisk spot on the shoulders of the figure just previous, both **A** and **B**. When the style line slashes opened up, the shoulder-collar back angle became much smaller. For the purists who worry that the center back grain of collar left and right will be different ... this is true. For that reason I would avoid making it in striped or plaid fabric and no one will notice.

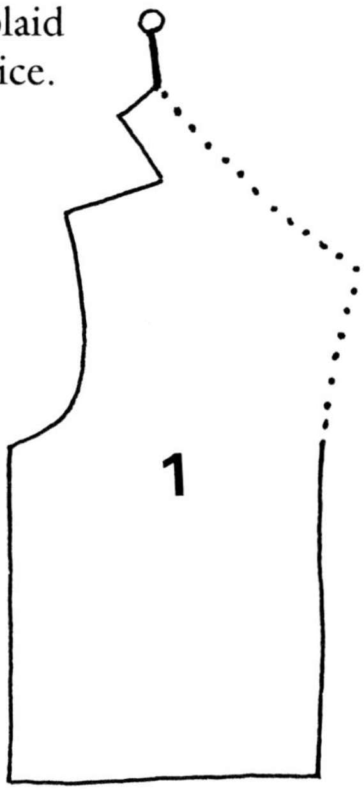

I considered alternative directions for slashing the fabric. For example, why not forget the slashes and instead, to keep the center back collars identical, use the top center back point as a pivot point where the straight pin is stuck. As illustrated here, the dark line of part **1** shows how much of the pattern remains unchanged, the dotted line shows the blouse left side

pattern. Part **2** shows the position of the pattern when it is pivoted at the pin to increase the collar style line.

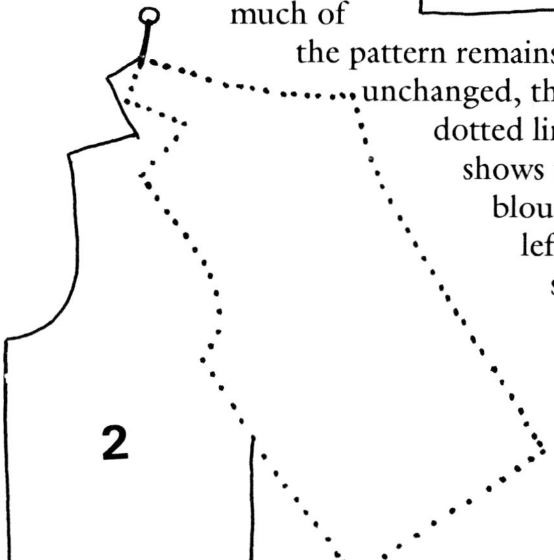

If you would make this up in fabric, you would find it wouldn't cascade as gracefully as figure **B** (on the previous page). Wherever you add to the pattern, it will show up in the fabric. This one is too deep between arrows and would be bulky around the neck. The previous slashed version added the fabric mainly in the outer style line staying more sleek in the neck area. For a better look at the finished blouse, check the blouses photographed for program 4. They are the same thing. The print version was a very inexpensive fabric made up as a test pattern before cutting out the expensive blue-purple sueded silk. When it was found to work out and drape beautifully, it was safe to cut out the better fabric without risk. Notice how the soft folds occur in exactly the same locations as the slashed and spread figure **B** (again, previous page). A test pattern is very comfortable to get answers without making expensive mistakes!

A special bonus has been included in this book ... this blouse center front and collar is the centerfold pattern. Remove it from this book to cut out and superimpose on a basic blouse pattern of your own design or purchase to duplicate the cover blouse, adjustable to any size. Directions are on the pattern sheet.

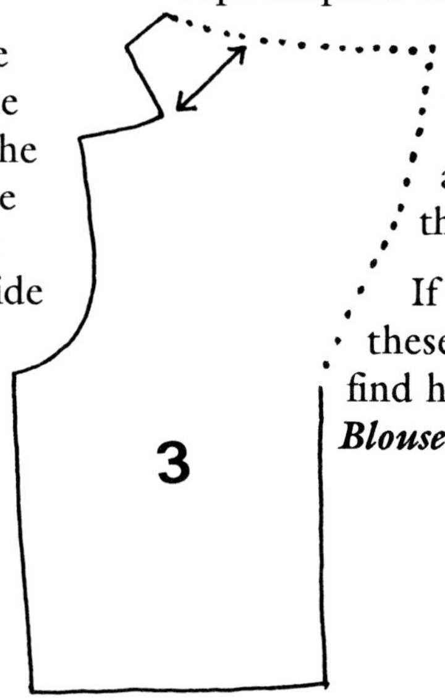

If you enjoyed figuring out these pattern design changes, find hundreds more in my book, *Blouse Pattern Pizazz*.

Program 4: Testing ... 1 2 3

The words you always hear when setting up a microphone system, we do the very same thing when first using a new pattern. We test it out to see:

1. Do I like it on me or do I want to modify the styling?
2. Does it fit perfectly or do I need to make some alterations?
3. Are there some difficult construction details I need to practice?

For all these reasons, we may need to make a test pattern and find the answers before directly cutting into the intended fabric. What fabric should we use? Do we need to go out and purchase some special yardage? Not necessarily as the perfect fabric may already be in our collections.

We have all bought fabric at some time and later wondered what in the world we were thinking! It looks terrible because our tastes change, or perhaps it has been around so long it has gone out of style. Maybe you even like it, but it was such a great bargain that very little money is at risk if it doesn't work out. Any of these would be good candidates if the fabric has a similar weight and hand as the final fabric for which the pattern will eventually be used. For example, denim is fairly inexpensive, but its firmness and thickness would be good before making the same pattern out of UltraSuede®. If it all works out correctly, finish up the test into a completed and wearable denim jacket. In the program 4 colored photo of the same blouse pattern, the very inexpensive print fabric was used as a test because it was thin, soft and drapey just like the sueded silk to eventually make the blouse. To use the "mistake" fabrics we bought is good because, even though we wouldn't care to finish them up and wear them, they accomplish a purpose in the test and we can quit feeling guilty for having bought them! Look for all these likely candidates first and whittle down your ugly fabric stash, only buying new fabric for a test when absolutely necessary. If I have no thought of ever wearing the test as a finished garment, I might also use up odds and ends of fabrics leftover from other projects. Each pattern piece can be cut from a different fabric, but again, try to use the right weight and hand in every piece of the mixture.

Does every new pattern need to be pretested? No. Look at the oversized green blouse photographed for program 2. This was a new pattern never before used and the fit was meant to be excessive. Instead of a test, I just measured the pieces and realized they were huge. Making it of the very thin soft silk, oversized was appropriate. Conversely, if the fit is meant to be very close and a perfectly altered pattern is necessary, I'll definitely make a test pattern.

Another test pattern photographed on the colored pages is the floral print linen jacket in program 12. This pattern was being considered for a sequined evening jacket ... an expensive risk. The flowered linen is quite wearable, but the pattern had faults so was later changed as evidenced in the slant of the shoulders, heightening the sleeve cap, and other alterations for a more flattering look. A test pattern is a very reassuring step to take when you have any doubts.

To begin, find only the main pattern pieces and cut them out. Lay them grain perfect on the fabric by measuring each end of the grain arrow out to the fabric edge to be sure they are exactly straight. A test pattern you want to make as quickly as possible, but unless you are accurate in cutting and constructing, it won't give you the true picture. All the little pieces (facings, pockets) need not be used unless you want to practice a particular technique. If you decide the test is wearable as an actual garment, you can always cut out these secondary pieces and finish it later.

Machine stitch it together with large stitches for easy alteration ripping out. Press as you construct just as you would an actual garment. Then try it on and look at it in the mirror with a very critical eye.

-- See if you find the cut flattering on you or if some small details should be changed to look better. Small changes like slightly relocating pockets or buttons might make a big difference in over all appearance.

-- Read the wrinkles. The garment should fit your body smoothly, wrinkle-free. If any wrinkles appear, where are they and what direction do they point? These are clues to any misfitting.

Any **vertical** wrinkle like this says one thing: the garment is hanging big and loose. If the printed description on the pattern envelope said "very loose fitting" expect to see this as the designer intended it. It's alright. Leave it alone. If it was intended to be a closely fit garment, the vertical wrinkle is saying make some bigger seams to take the fit in smaller. Pin in where it seems appropriate and check to see if the look is improved. Gathers, pleats are also vertical wrinkles, but intentional, not misfits.

Horizontal wrinkles say "too tight." Picture a skirt or slacks with horizontal wrinkles across the tummy. These are unflattering and obviously saying let out the side seams. Sometimes this also occurs across the back shoulders when shoulders are broad and pulling the fabric. Think of a woman with a large bust and the fabric is straining with horizontal wrinkles in the area. Please leave some ease as it make the body look so much better. How much ease depends on the fabric used (heavy fabrics can be tighter than thin fabrics), the type garment, and the swinging fashion pendulum. For the past many years, we've been wearing oversized clothing, but now many garments are fitting more closely.

Diagonal wrinkles tell you that the shape or set is wrong as those in the illustration. These diagonal wrinkles appear in every blouse or tee shirt you put on. Is anything wrong? Not in these type garments which are perfectly flat in shape when you have a shapely body inside. These diagonals are inevitable and quite acceptable. The fabric is thin and soft and it looks just fine.

Picture those same wrinkles in a fitted suit jacket. This is not acceptable. Structured garments like this are interfaced, lined and the diagonal wrinkle says you are shapelier than the suit. Alterations are needed.

"Miss" patterns are meant for "B" bra cups. If you are a "C" or larger, you need extra length and extra width. The

Diagonal wrinkles are not acceptable in a fitted jacket

Diagonal wrinkles in the back are problems dozens of viewers have written me about. This problem is compounded by the collar which stands away from the back neck. A third fault is that the lower hem pulls up at center back. Where those diagonal wrinkles occur, the base of them out at the armscye seems to have extra fabric tempting you to stitch them into darts (resist the temptation). The center back is simply too short.

easiest alterations and the most flattering fit can be found in a jacket with princess lines. This is the pattern to purchase.

Princess

The alterations are pictured as made across the center front piece lengthening it $7/8$" for each cup size beyond "B". The side front is lengthened the same amount over the bust, tapering to nothing at the side seam. Extra width is also added to the bust of the side piece, tapering to original seam above and below. Book 4 dealt with the bust problem more extensively so will not be elaborated upon further here.

Diagonal wrinkles almost always point to the source of the problem. In this case it is a rounded back at the center of the shoulder area. It is actually a matter of posture. The side view shows these problems more clearly. This points out the fact that you need to look at yourself in the mirror from several views for thorough analysis and understanding.

As you look at this side view, if you would force yourself to stand very straight, the problems would disappear. The collar would close in on your neck, the diagonal folds would leave the armscye, and the lower hem would lengthen and touch your body rather than standing out. This is a forced solution however, and we must deal with reality instead. We cannot make our bodies fit the clothes. The clothing must be altered to hang beautifully on the body when it is standing comfortably in its accustomed posture.

The solution will be to add more length where the back is rounded, as the previous arrow indicates (bottom right page 18). In that test pattern fabric that doesn't matter, slash horizontally from one side to the other right at that curve which is also the location of the wrinkles, as illustrated. As the slashed fabric opens up, the jacket fits beautifully! Magically, the collar goes in place, the hem drops down at center back, the diagonals disappear. Have someone tape across the opening when it hangs correctly. This is to preserve the correction while you take off your jacket and make the identical alteration on your pattern, mounting and taping it to some paper.

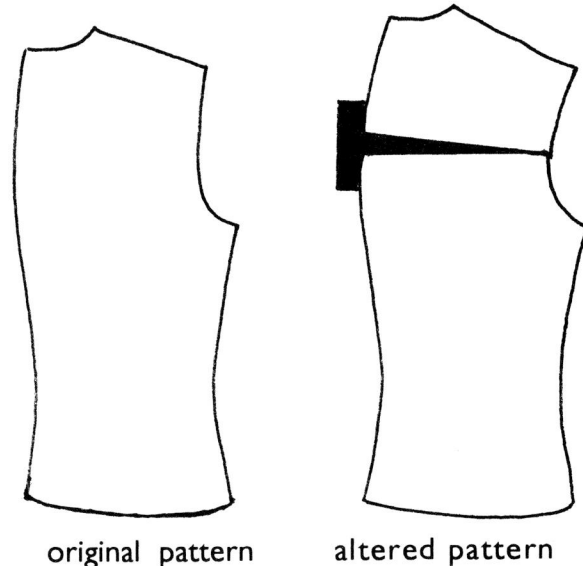

original pattern   altered pattern

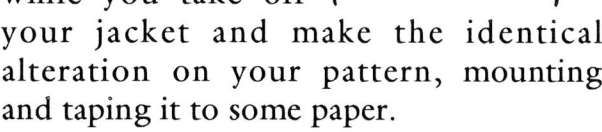

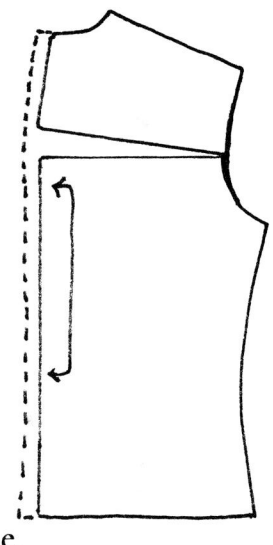

If the pattern you have is cut on a back fold rather than with a seam, the test fabric alteration will still be the same. Your paper pattern, however, will need to be corrected to incorporate the extra length in the open slash. Then a seam allowance will need to be added since a fold (straight line) is no longer possible.

Notice how the center back seam now curves more than the original. This can only be done with a center back seam so look for patterns that feature the seam. On you the fit will be much nicer.

Sometimes only part of a garment will need to be tested. If a sleeve is suspected of being too tight, perhaps only that one piece will need to be made up and altered. Or maybe just a dress bodice will need a test pattern, the skirt not being a problem area.

Whatever are your needs or your body's demands, a test pattern may be the way to find solutions. It takes a little more time, but is a wonderful "insurance policy" to eliminate worry. Whatever are your figure faults, a perfectly fit garment will minimize them and improve your overall appearance.

Program 5: Embellishing The Truth

Truth of the matter is I have some fabrics I don't like. Obviously I loved them when I bought them ... but much later I couldn't imagine what in the world made me think I wanted them. You've done the same? We could throw them out of course, but that's admitting defeat. Let's instead accept a difficult challenge. Come explore with me some of the ways we can redesign that fabric. Let's embellish the truth!

One fabric I bought was so unique. There were big splotches all over, kind of like a tie-dyed fabric. It is being worn by the model in the color photo for program 5. Within a month after I bought this "one-of-a-kind" fabric, I saw it in every fabric shop I entered. What can we do to once again make it unique?

Cabling

This is a fun process using your machine in a way that might be new. For this decorative stitching choose a heavy thread or cord. Some of those which work well are pearl cotton, ribbon floss, yarn, most of the heavy novelty threads you would use in your serger might be tried. This requires working on machine and when finished, this heavy thread will be in little pebble-looking loops on the top surface of your fabric.

Probably too heavy to sew through the needle, it will instead be used in the bobbin. The top thread can be any kind of sewing thread of the same color. Because the cord is heavy, a whole lot won't fit on the bobbin and it shouldn't have too much cord per bobbin. Too much wouldn't let the bobbin turn easily in the case. The solution is to wind several bobbins before you start the cable stitch process.

When inserting the bobbin in the bobbin case, **BYPASS** the tension spring and just thread the cord through a little hole in the bobbin case so it moves easily without any restraint. Put the case in place in the machine, bring the cord up through the throat plate opening.

This will be free motion stitching so lower the feed teeth and remove the presser foot. If you have a free arm machine, attach the platform to make a broader base for keeping the embroidery hoop flat.

The fabric must be taut so insert it in an embroidery hoop, right side down. Remember the bobbin cord or novelty threads are wanted on the fabric right side, so it needs to be down toward the bobbin and you will work looking at the wrong side of the fabric as you stitch.

Lower the presser bar and you may bring the bobbin cord up through the fabric (the wrong side). Or you can also leave the cord underneath, later cutting it or dealing with it in some way. If your fabric is closely woven, it will be difficult to bring the ends through. In that case, when finished, merely cut it short and dab on a little seam sealant.

With the machine set on straight stitch, move the hoop around to create whatever design you please ... as sparse or thick as you prefer. The splotchy design on my fabric showed through to the backside, so I followed the outlines moving quickly back and forth and around. It looks

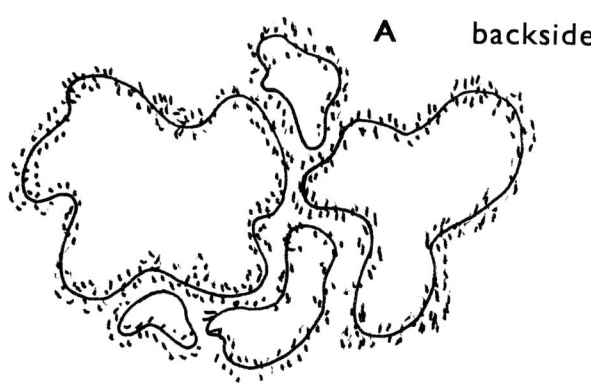

A backside

like these little stitches. To turn it over and look at the right side, all the curly little loops of **B** showed, making it quite interesting.

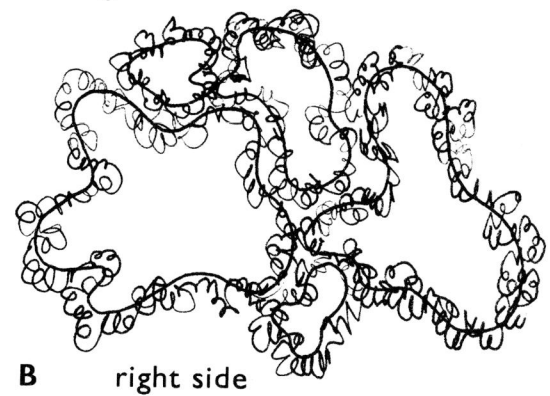

B right side

Of course try this first on a scrap to see if you actually like it. If after you evaluate the results you decide to apply the technique to a garment, fine. Possibly you'll decide it's not worth continuing, but you can chalk it up to a good learning experience.

Elastic

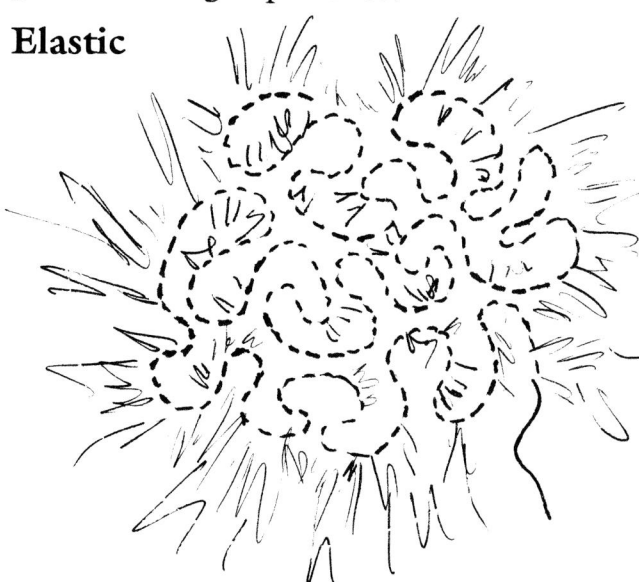

Use the same cabling technique as above with elastic thread in the bobbin instead; again, no tension. With the fabric in a hoop and **right side up**, stitch moving the hoop around for a passamenterie design. When it is released from the hoop, it puckers up delightfully producing the elasticized fabric seen in some swimsuits, or on a dress yoke, or the waist and upper hip part of a skirt.

Try straight lines of this stitching, holding the fabric out taut with a presser foot, but not using a hoop. The heavier the fabric, the more rows are needed. This technique is frequently used on thin fabrics as the waistline of a pull-on skirt or the lower band of an over blouse. When your hands release the tautly held fabric, it gathers up beautifully. I've seen this technique on many designer outfits.

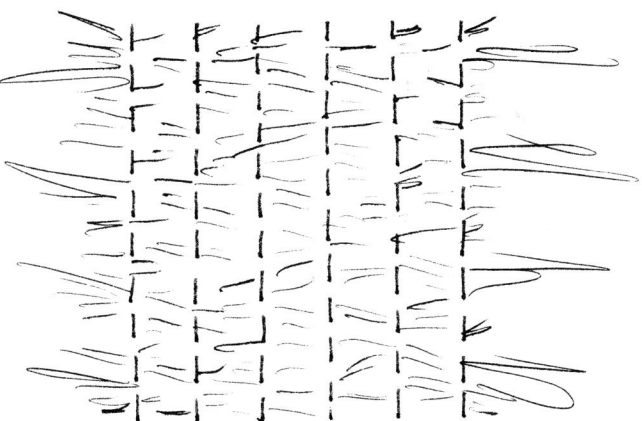

Another "truth" (translate: ugly fabric) I bought thinking the colors were so subtle. Now I look at it and think how incredibly boring it is ... a dirty grey chiffon print! If it can be rescued at all, perhaps it will be by an iridescent thread for reflected rainbows. Metallic threads would lend sparkle and bring it back to life. Try both and maybe even make it wearable!

Metallic Machine Embroidery

Either of these threads might be used with a medium sized needle. If the threads tend to shred and break as some brands might, try a larger needle or reverse the operation. Wind the thread on the bobbin and stitch from the fabric wrong side so the metallic bobbin thread shows on the right side.

These thin threads will not cable stitch the way the heavy cords will; therefore, install the bobbin the standard way using the bobbin case tension spring. Again a hoop will be needed to hold the fabric taut. No foot is needed as this will be free motion embroidery, so it may be removed. On zigzag, outline designs or fill in the designs completely as this figure illustrates. If this improves the fabric and you apply it to a garment, begin with designs near your face so it can be worn with a little bit of embellishment. If you then have the time, expand the embroidery to wider areas. Anytime you machine embroider, you will need a hoop to keep fabric taut unless you use a stabilizer under the fabric, later tearing it away.

Maybe you love what you produce on the scraps and want to then proceed with the whole garment. Maybe it doesn't thrill you, but you've still profited. You've learned another way to use your machine and taught yourself a fun process to store in the back of your mind to resurrect at some future time on another project.

Program 6: *I Love to Sew With My Feet with guest Jan Saunders*

We mean presser feet, of course! Jan is a very talented, very knowledgeable guest who has written numerous books on using your machine to its fullest capabilities. Some gems from Jan follow:

Button Reed Used As A Wedge

Sewing up and over heavy seams on a jean hem or attaching a belt loop is tough because the foot stalls on the way up and coasts on the way down the thickness. This happens because the foot is not level with the feed dogs.

Use the button reed as a wedge under the heel of the foot as you approach a thickness, and under the toes as you come off the thickness.

1. As the toes tip up, stop with the needle in the fabric and lift the foot. Slip the wedge under the heel and lower the presser foot.

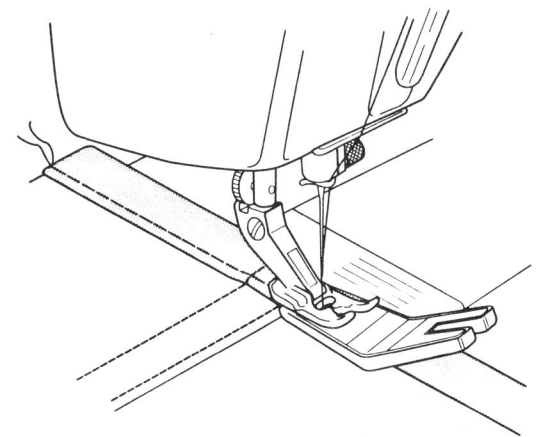

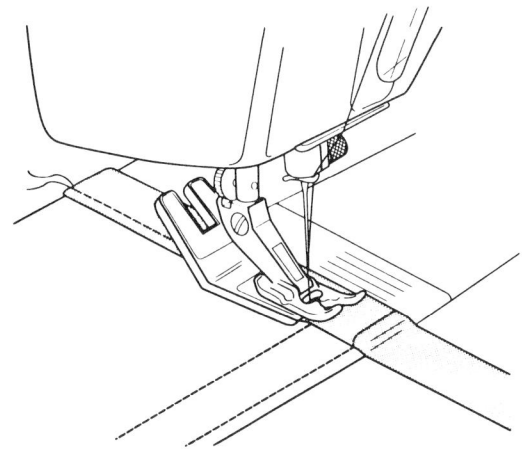

2. Stitch across the thickness until the toes begin to tip down. Stop with the needle in the fabric and lift the foot again.

3. Slip wedge under the toes and take a few stitches until the back of the foot is off the thickness. Remove wedge.

This technique prevents stitch distortion and keeps the needle from breaking on the foot as it pivots on and off the thickness.

When starting a seam or topstitching a heavy fabric, place needle at the edge of the fabric and the reed under the heel of the foot. This way the foot doesn't have to climb uphill to start sewing.

Hemstitch Fork

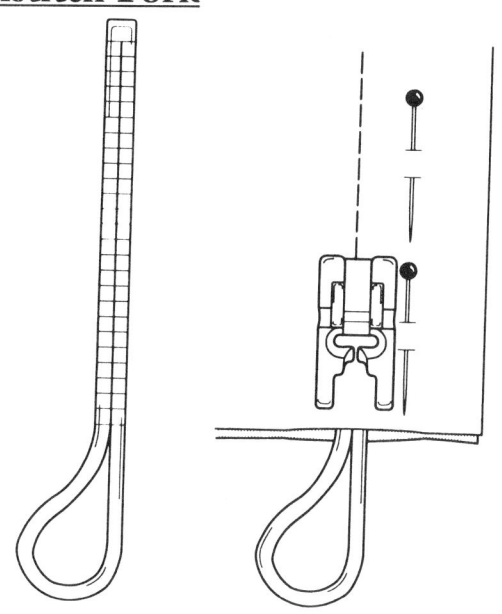

23

This accessory is available through your local Viking dealer and can be used on any brand of sewing machine. It looks like a large bobby pin and is used for fagoting with the straight stitch.

Straight stitch about 9 per inch using a standard zigzag foot and an 80/12 universal needle. Loosen the top tension slightly.

1. Pin your fabric, right sides together, placing pins parallel to, and $1/8$" (3mm) from the raw edge.
2. Slip the fork between the layers of fabric so the loop of the fork is toward you and the fork is snugged up to the pins.
3. Place the fork under the needle, put the needle down between the lines, then put the foot down. Stitch slowly to the loop in the fork. Stop with the needle down, lift the foot, and pull the fork toward you.
4. Put the foot back down, stitch to the loop, pull the fork toward you. Continue until the line of stitching is complete.
5. Remove the fork and press the seam open. The folds will separate and you will see a thread ladder between them. If desired, topstitch seam allowances on either side of the ladders.

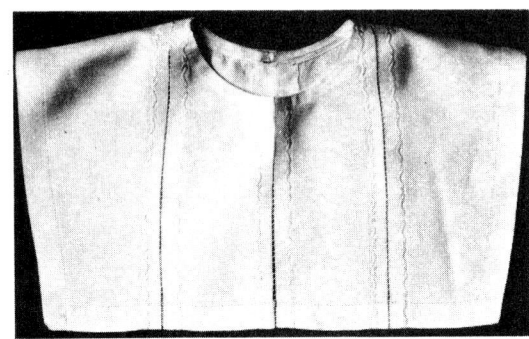

You can use this method to join seams on baby clothes, French hand-sewn (by machine) blouses, collars, pocket tops, yokes, or anywhere you may want an interesting seam. Piece fabrics together for a collar, tablecloth, or front tab.

Piping Foot

The underside of the piping foot has wide groove designed to cover cord used to edge upholstery and pillow seams. It is also used to insert piping. Although you can use the zipper foot for either purpose, the piping foot makes it easier, and the stitching is more accurate.

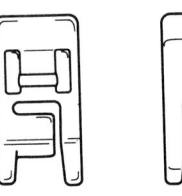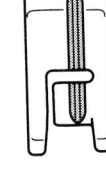

top   underside

To cover cord, cut the fabric on the bias the width of cord plus $1\,1/4$" (3.2cm) or unfold bias tape. Sandwich cord in the fabric or bias tape, then place it under the foot so the cord fits in the groove. Decenter the needle so the line of stitching snugs up against the cording and stitch.

To attach the finished cord or piping evenly, and without catching it in the seam, this foot is a must.

Great ideas for applications are piping yokes and pockets, tote bags, handbags, backpacks, pillows, hemlines, or slipcovers. You can use it when reupholstering ... anywhere there is a seam. Also use the piping foot for an exposed zipper application.

Bias Binder

A bias binder is used for applying flat or prefolded bias tape, binding or trim, Available for most machines, the bias binder has a funnel and guide to fold the binding over the base fabric before it reaches the needle.

Some bias binders are used only with a straight stitch; others can be used with a zigzag or decorative stitch. Others

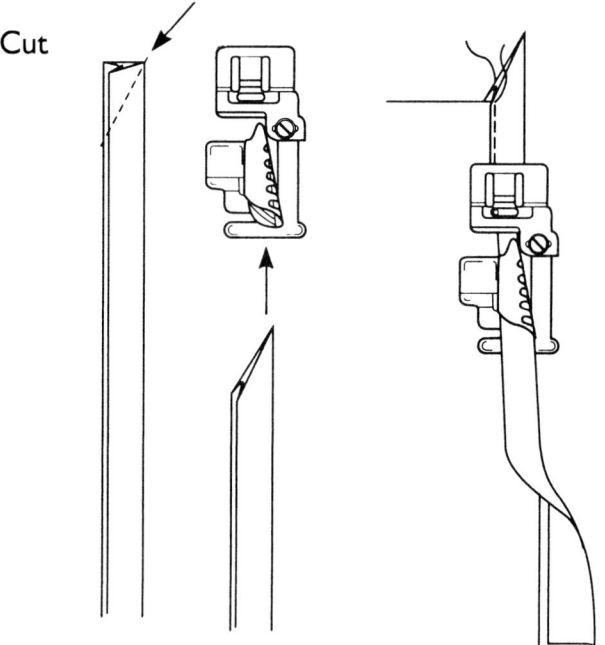

are even adjustable to accommodate varying widths of prefolded tape.

1. Unfold 3" (7.5cm) of one end of a length of bias tape and press flat.
2. On the pressed end, fold tape in half the long way and make a **V**-shaped cut so the point of the cut is at the fold (observe diagram above).
3. With the binder off the machine, thread tape through the funnel so the point of the cut is to the right. **NOTE:** If you are having trouble threading the funnel, use a hand needle and doubled thread to stitch through the point of the **V** and pull the point through the funnel.
4. Put binder on machine and pull the feed end of tape so it extends about 2" (5cm) behind the foot.
5. Slip the base fabric into the slot in the center of the funnel.
6. Adjust your needle position so the needle stitches inside the folded edge of the tape.

This can be used to bind the edges of double-faced quilted fabric for placemats or an unlined jacket. Stitch on bias tape or Seams Great® for a Hong Kong seam finish or hem.

Braiding Feet

Narrow Braiding Foot. Sometimes referred to as a narrow cording foot, this foot is not usually standard, but I feel it's a necessity. The top of the foot has a guide to hold narrow cord, such as pearl cotton, yarn, or cordonnet. The underside has a narrow channel behind the needle which flairs out at the heel, enabling you to stitch around curves and corners smoothly.

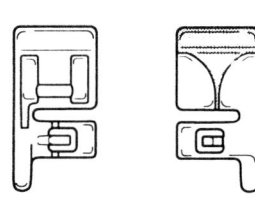

top   underside

Uses for this foot include, cording an edge that will be satin-stitched later. To gather, use this foot to zigzag over a cord so you don't catch the cord in the stitch. Create your own fabric by using a solid base fabric and couch interesting yarn in a plaid, stripe, or scrolled design.

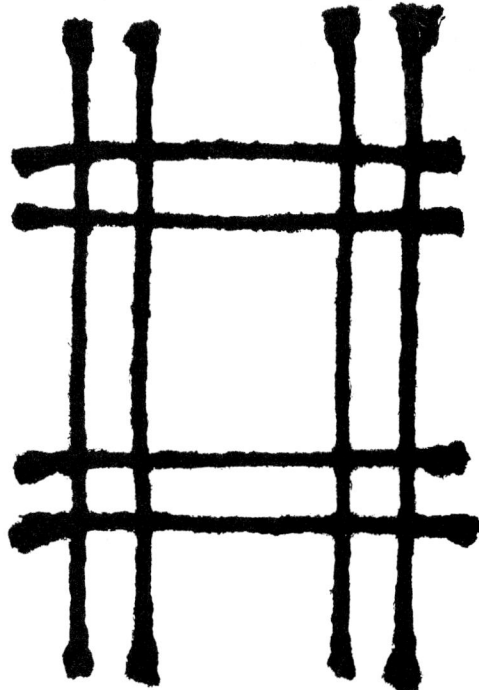

Outline an applique with yarn or cord by straight stitching through it.

25

Because the clip or guide holds the cord in place, you can stitch in any direction and be assured of stitching through the cord to anchor it properly. For truly invisible results, use nylon monofilament thread top and bobbin. This way all you see is the cord or yarn and not the stitches.

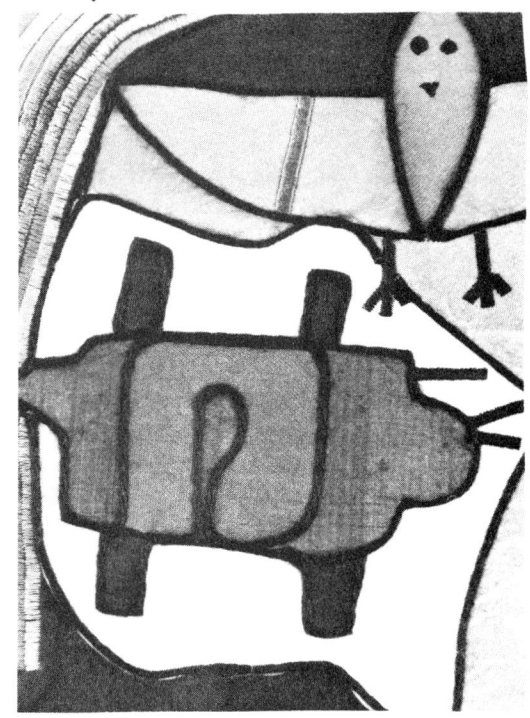

Standard Braiding Foot: The standard braiding foot has an opening in front of the needle large enough to accommodate middy or soutache braid. Some braiding feet have an adjustable guide or hole for varying weights of braid, yarn, or cord.

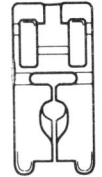 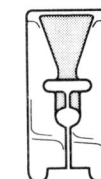

top   underside

The standard braiding foot works on the same principle as the narrow braiding foot, but the channel on the underside is wider and feeds the braid straight.

Try embellishing jackets, children's clothing, and costumes with braid, or couch over heavy yarn, cord, or trim.

Gathering Foot

This foot gathers light- to medium-weight fabric automatically while sewing. The underside is raised behind the needle and there is slot in front of the needle.

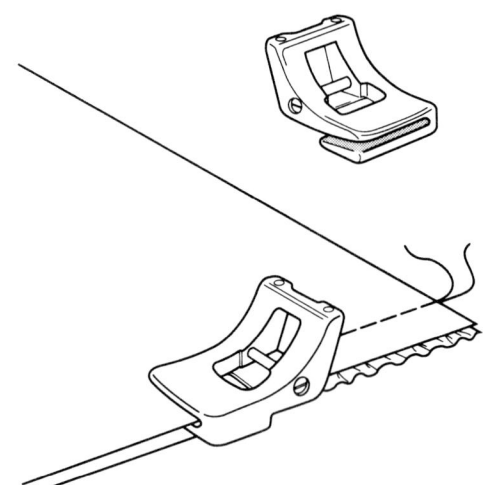

To use this foot, set your machine for a straight stitch. The amount the fabric gathers is determined by the stitch length and upper thread tension. Use a long stitch and a tighter tension for a lot of heavy gathers. Use a short stitch and normal tension for finer gathers.

To gather and sew a ruffle onto a flat piece of fabric, place the fabric to be gathered under the foot, right side up, and put the foot down. Slip the flat piece into the slot with the right side down and stitch. Everything is stitched in one step. However, the stitching may not be straight and even. Therefore, you may want to gather the fabric first and attach it in a second step.

To determine how much gathering you need, stitch a test piece. Start with a strip of fabric 10"(25.5cm) long. This way, if the fabric gathers to 5" (12.75cm), you know to use a two to one ration ... or use a 50" (125cm) length of ruffle to attach to a 25" (62.5cm) waistband.

Use this to gather ruffles for children's clothing, curtains, dust ruffles, tablecloths, or blouses.

To use all those wonderful feet that came with your machine, or which are available for purchase at your machine dealer makes any task so much easier. Also accept the challenge of finding on your own new ways these feet can help you.

Thank you to

Chilton Book Company
Radnor, Pennsylvania 19087

And most especially thank you
Jan Saunders
Speed Sewing Limited
5725 Ballymead Boulevard
Dublin, Ohio 43017

Bibliography

Saunders, Jan, Teach Yourself to Sew Better, A Step-By-Step Guide to Your Sewing Machine, 4 color, Chilton, 1990.

Saunders, Jan, Teach Yourself to Sew Better, A Step-By-Step Guide to Your Bernina, 4 color, Chilton, 1991.

Saunders, Jan, Teach Yourself to Sew Better, A Step-By-Step Guide to Your New Home Sewing Machine, 4 color, Chilton, 1991.

Saunders, Jan, Teach Yourself to Sew Better, A Step-By-Step Guide to Your Viking, 4 color, Chilton, 1990.

Saunders, Jan, Sew, Serge, Press -- Speed Tailoring in the Ultimate Sewing Center, 4 color, Chilton, 1989.

Program 1

Program 2

Program 3

Program 4

Program 5

Program 6

Program 7

Program 8

Program 9

Program 10

Program 13

Program 12

The Sewing Connection Book V Template for C Cascade Ruffle Closure.

This pattern is meant to be pinned to a basic blouse pattern of your own in order to change it to the same look as pictured. It is a variation of a shawl collar. Put away your collar and facing pattern pieces as this will substitute for them, forming a small stand up collar in back. The pattern you use should have a standard back and front joined by a shoulder seam. **Do not** use a pattern with a yoke.

Before beginning, lay a tape measure on edge on the back neck stitching line of your blouse. Compare your measurement with the template stitching line measurement ($3\frac{1}{4}$"). Adjust the template longer or shorter so it matches yours.

Measure your front blouse pattern length from the shoulder-neck stitching line dot down to the bottom. Adjust the template ($25\frac{5}{8}$") longer or shorter so it matches up with your pattern.

Trace the template pieces on pattern tracer or cut these out and use as your patterns.

Cut one layer sheer interfacing for each template, sew in or fusible. If fusible, cut with the **fusible side down** while template print is up.

Cut one facing layer of each template with the **fabric right side down**. Fuse or staystitch the interfacing to the facing. This facing layer is also the inner collar.

Pin the templates to your pattern (one at a time) to form the blouse front-outer collar units.

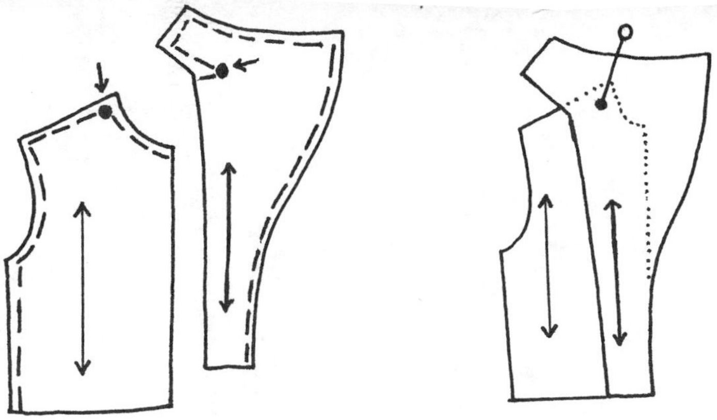

First put a pin in the neck-shoulder dot of right template on top of the same neck-shoulder point of your pattern front. Pivot the template until its grain arrow is parallel with the grain arrow of your pattern. The center front lines may be slightly off because of pattern variations, but it will not matter. Pin securely and cut one layer of your blouse right front. Unpin the template.

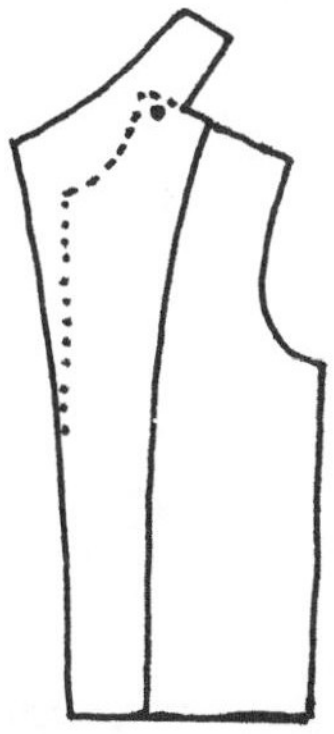

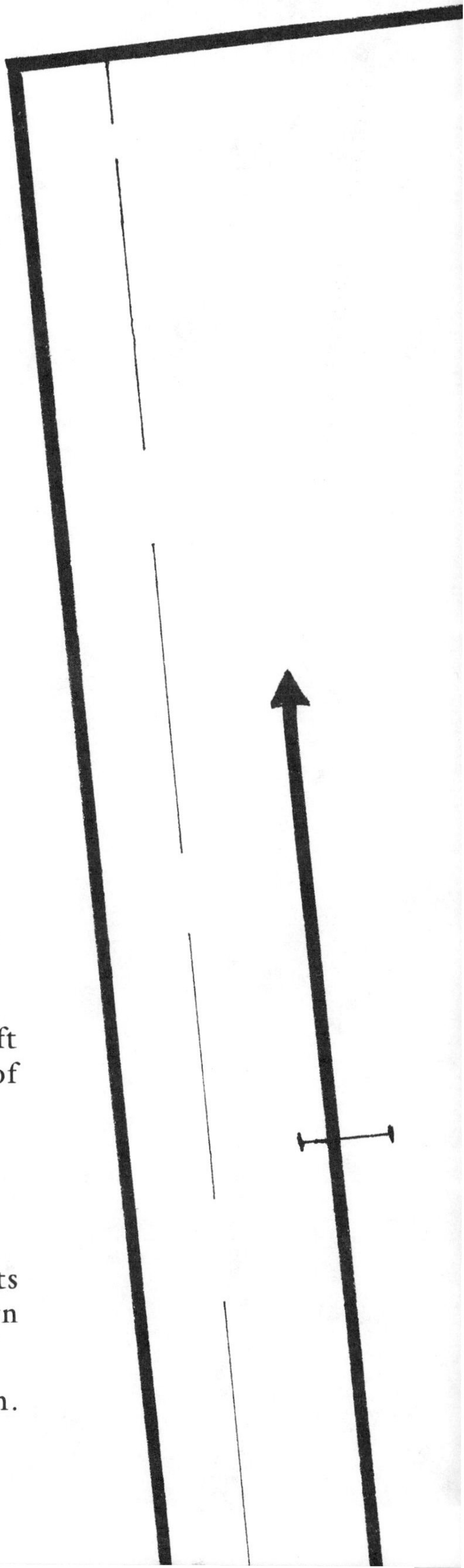

Turn the pattern over so it is in the left front position. Pin the left template to it in the same manner as above. Cut out one layer of the blouse left front.

Mark the neck-shoulder dot on all four fabric layers (two fronts and two facings) and stitch small reinforcement stitches as shown on template. Slash to the point of reinforcement.

Stitch the center back seam in the two facing pieces. Press open. Serge or hem the long vertical edge of each facing to finish.

Staystitch the blouse back neckline $1/2$"

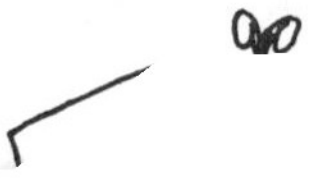

Stitch the blouse fronts together on the center back seam. Press open. The grain of these two little areas is different as explained in the chapter on shawl collars. It will be alright.

Stitch the front and back shoulder seams together up to the neck dots. Backstitch at those points. Accuracy here is very important. Now all that remains is the back neck seam, so stitch it. Finish shoulder seams and press shoulders toward the front, back neck seam up toward the stand up collar.

Stitch the facing-inner collar unit to the blouse-outer collar unit all around the edge. Trim, turn, press. Finish the back neck by turning under the inner collar seam and whipping down by hand. Do the same with facing upper edges on the shoulder seams.

Stitch buttonholes as marked on right template. The buttons will be stitched approximately where marked on left template, but may vary somewhat. The fact that they are close together while buttonholes are farther apart is what causes the cascade ruffle.

Copyright 1992 © Shirley Adams

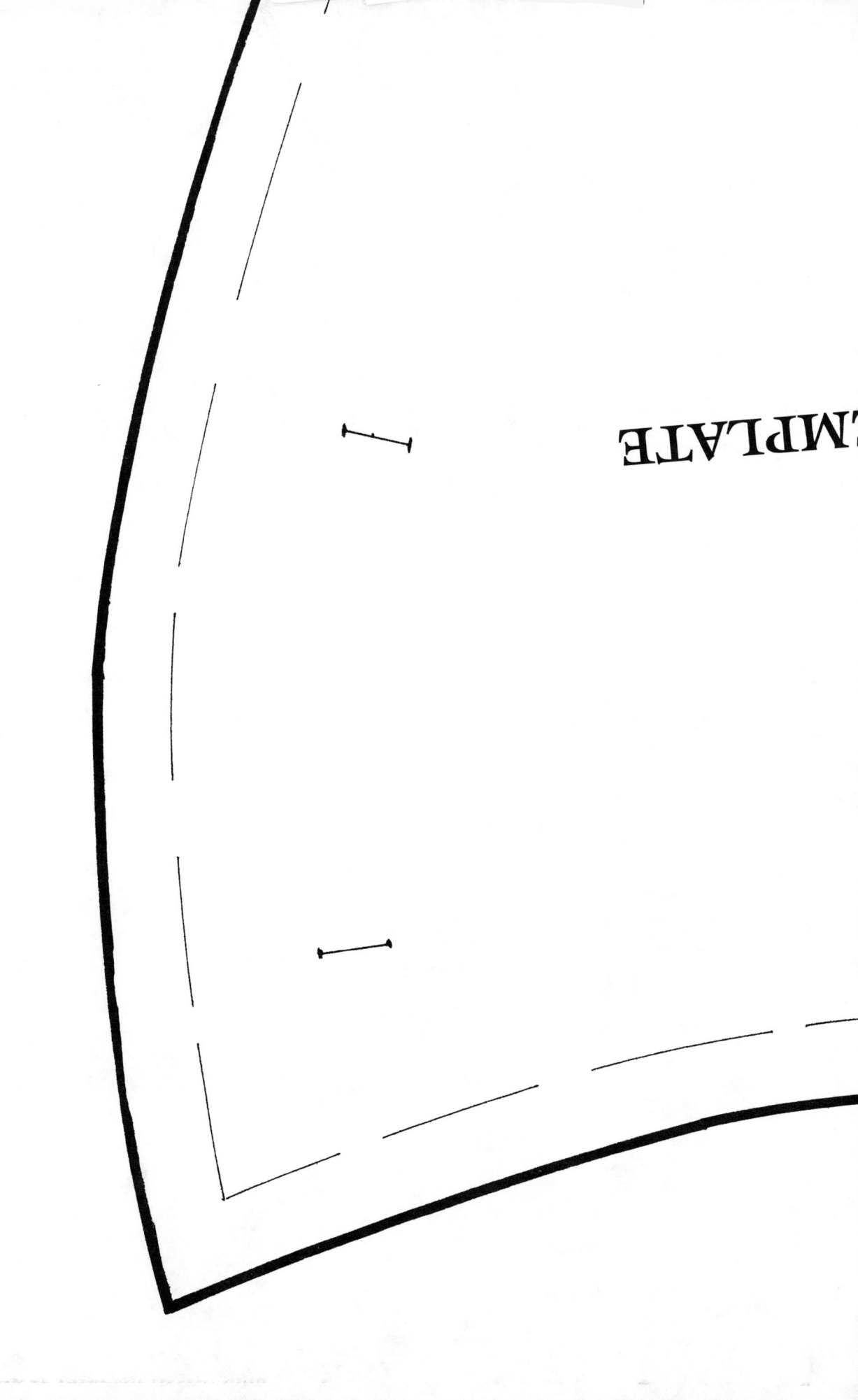

Program 7: Terrific Tubes

Whether the end use is for decorative corded belts and other pretty touches, or whether it is a utilitarian feature like a buttonloop ... fabric tubes can be very useful. They are so easy to make it's unbelievable! But mainly it's such fun it becomes addictive and you search for ways to use them.

To start your imagination on a creative path, picture these possibilities:

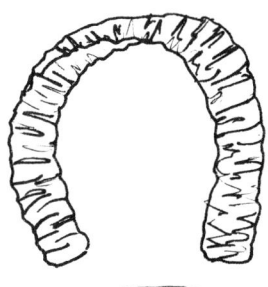

- A plastic headband becomes much more interesting when covered with a tube of gathered fabric coordinated with the outfit worn.

- A visor band, adjustable in size with a snap-on bill. A quick little accessory is fun to make.

- For the man who invariably drops gravy on his tie, a reversible one for a quick change may be just the ticket. A tube need not be the same width its entire length and this can work out very nicely.

- A fastidious little girl might be delighted with shoe laces from the same fabric as her dress. Metal end pieces to clamp on the narrow tubes can be found in craft stores or notions departments.

- A multi strand braided necklace is a sporty accessory which goes well over a simple tee top. Mix coordinating prints in the fabrics chosen. Earrings and bracelets are similarly made.

- On a slightly heavier scale, a belt would be wider and much firmer in the end pieces. Velcro® would be one choice for fastening. These last few ideas would probably involve some firm padding in the tubes such as provided by upholstery welting.

Many more corded belt specifics are instructed in my book *Belt Bazaar*.

- An interesting bag can be made of a combination of different size tubes. The end panel tubes can be 2" or more wide, fabric cut

on the straight or bias. These tubes are padded with fleece, bridge-stitched together until of a sufficient size piece. The center panel is a solid fabric background covered by a lattice of smaller tubes staystitched in place on the ends. The two end panels are then seamed to the center to complete each side of the bag.

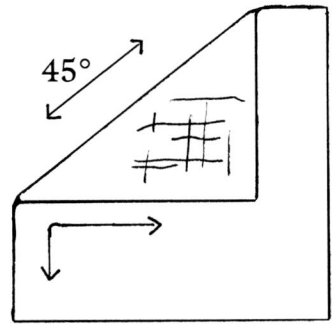

The top rim of the bag is a tube covering a metal framework (purchased in craft departments). The strap is a straight cut strip, 1 1/2" wide and padded for firmness and comfort.

Are you beginning to think of how tubes could be incorporated into your sewing? Then let's get to the beginning and first sew some tubes.

If your fabric is woven, fold a corner over to produce a 45° angle for your cut strip. This is necessary for the nicest appearance if the tube will curve or move freely on the finished garment. If it will be sewn flat in a rigid formation it may be cut on the straight as it would not have a ripple concern. If the fabric is knit, cutting it crosswise produces the best appearance.

Cut your strips twice the width needed plus two seam allowances. These seams may be narrow if the strip is of reasonable width. If it is going to be a really thin tube, tiny seams are difficult to control. Cut larger seams and, after stitching, trim the seams down narrower before turning right side out.

It is better to use rather small stitches if the tube will have any stretch (woven bias or knit crosswise) as this provides more elasticity than larger stitches. The thread will be less likely to break when turned or pulled.

Mass produce fabric tubes easily with the help of a Fasturn®, a brass tube which is as fascinating to observe its incredible simplicity as it is to marvel at its efficiency. Several sizes of the tubes are available. Use a size slightly smaller than the fabric tube opening. Its smooth surface easily slides inside the fabric. The fabric gathers up as is necessary while pushing its length onto the Fasturn®.

When the whole fabric tube is on the outside of the Fasturn®, fold the fabric end over the tube end. Insert the wire coil down the tube and turn it clockwise to engage the wire end hook or coil securely through the fabric. Then pull the wire back out and the fabric tube will turn itself right side out while being pulled through the Fasturn's® interior. When first starting to pull it through, open up the seam allowances and the rest will automatically open as it is pulled. This produces a fabric tube which has the bulk nicely distributed and the seam will be flat as though it has been pressed.

At the start of the fabric tube's turning, insert a cord, yarns, upholstery welting or other stuffing if appropriate. This is easily done by touching its end to the fabric opening as it is being turned. It

deftly pulls the cording right with the fabric, neatly covering it within the fabric tube. To then disengage the wire coil, rotate it counter clockwise.

Elastic can be inserted instead of cord for a stretchy, flat, gathered tube. This might be a fun idea for suspenders on a child's garment. They fit well now, but will then "grow" for next year's wearing. Before pulling the elastic through the tube while turning the fabric right side out, stitch a double length of yarn to the other elastic end. This is so the elastic won't get lost inside of the long fabric.

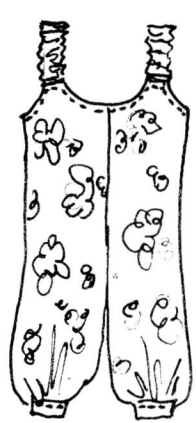

When turned, the yarn can be pulled to bring the elastic end out to the fabric end. Stitch across each end to secure the elastic permanently.

Button Loops

The fabric will be cut on the bias if woven, width depending on appropriate size in end product. For a silky blouse or dress fabric, I want this tube to be as slim as possible. To try to stitch a very narrow strip is very difficult so cut it possibly 1 1/4" wide. Fold right sides together and stitch as close to the fold as the tube width is to be. Trim the wide seam allowances and turn right side out. It will stretch longer because of the bias cut. This means it will also become narrower, and as narrow as possible is the goal. It may stretch and slim more willingly with moisture (steam iron or spray bottle). Pin each stretched out end to the ironing board padding and let dry. Mass produce all the button loops needed in one long strand if possible, then cut into pieces afterwards to stitch in place between layers of garment.

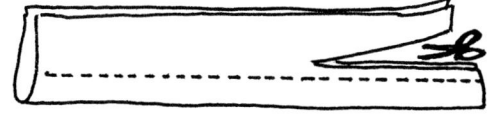

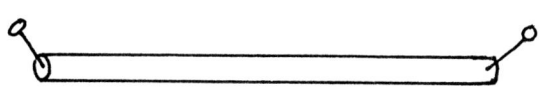

If "beefing up" the size would be better, it can be made wider and turned over cording.

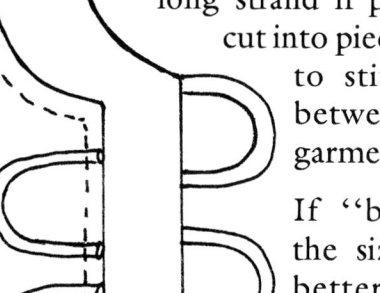

Chinese Ball Buttons

A small button (1/2") needs a 1/4" fabric tube filled with two yarns. A 1" ball button requires a 3/8" tube and a soft upholstery cord or welting for filler. It should be approximately 12" long per button. To tie the knot which produces the ball follow the diagrams:

Weave #3 over, under, over, etc. then gradually work it all around, pulling ends tighter until it shapes up into a ball. Cut off the cord ends and sew flat to the underside with a few hand stitches. These work well used as a button with the buttonloop or as part of a frog closure.

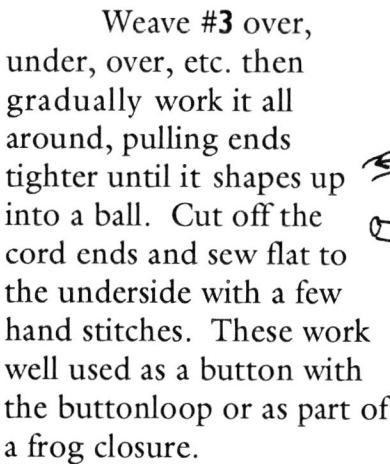
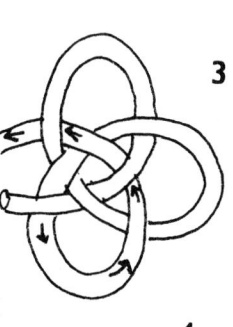

30

Vest or Jacket

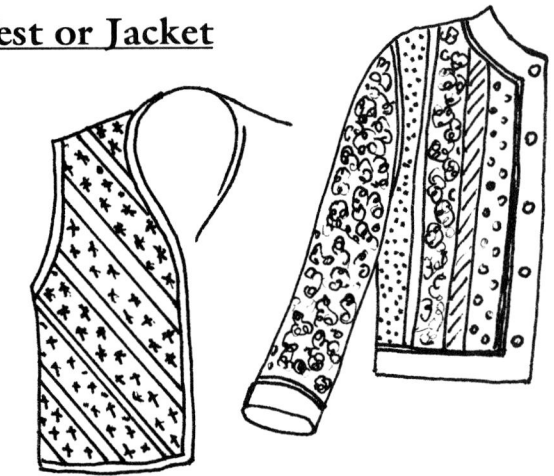

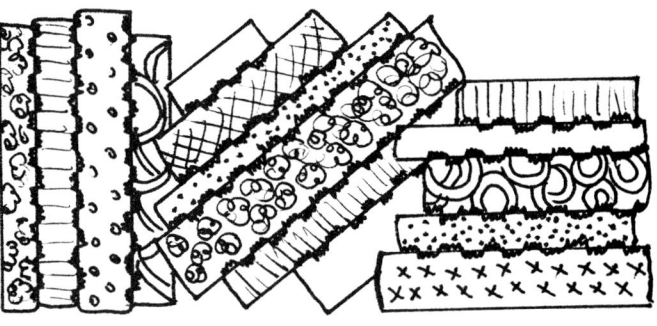

The strips of fabric for the tubes can be cut on straight grain. The object is to "build" a piece of fabric large enough to fit the pattern piece and cut it out. Repeat for all pattern pieces, then construct the jacket. This will be a reversible if seams are all finished off so inside and outside are equally pretty. To make this job quicker, usually only the fronts are tubes, backs and sleeves just being two layers of fabric.

Cut the strips the proper length and desired width using a rotary cutter. The quickest way is to layer fleece down on your cutting surface first, then two layers of fabric, right sides together on top. For a little more interest, these strips need not all be the same width but can vary as you, the designer, would like. Use a straight edge to cut through all layers at once.

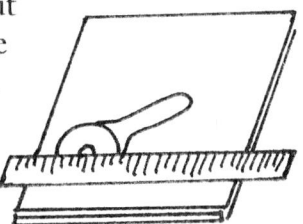

Stitch the strip layers together, fleece on bottom, a small seam on each long side. Insert the Fasturn® between **fabric** layers. Turn, press, and be ready to connect the strips by a bridging stitch on your machine. Plan the direction of the joined strips (this you needed to plan in advance as it determines

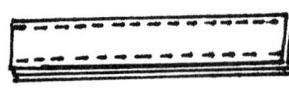

the length of them). Arrange them all first on a table to decide which will be placed adjacent to which. Turn back and forth to see which side of each should be up or down.

Whatever zigzag type stitch you use to connect these strips together, the job will be made easier by using a joining foot. Not usually one automatically included with your machine, it can be purchased separately from your machine dealer. It has a projection under the foot which rides between the two strips promoting a perfectly regulated row of joining stitches.

After cutting out and constructing your garment, bind the outer edges with bias to finish.

Other Uses

• Consider enlarging a sleeve as well as making it cooler for summer by a series of tubes bridging the space created. Bias tape on the underside would cover the raw edges.

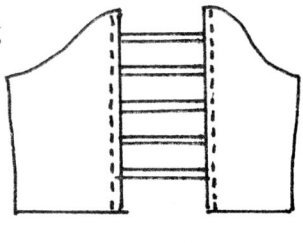

I recently saw a long sleeved version of this, beautifully done in a soft silky fabric. The soft tubes gently swagged the sleeve length.

Think of tubes used as spaghetti straps on sundresses or formal wear. Consider several used across the back as illustrated here. Or perhaps use on both shoulders interwoven into a lattice back.

What really caught my eye recently was a multi-thousand dollar jacket which looked like New Year's Eve with confetti and streamers covering it. The confetti will be attached "jewels" sewn on, but those streamers will be multi-colored tubes. Experimenting for the same look, I discovered that to stitch the silky bias cut foldovers in a wavy thick-thin pattern would

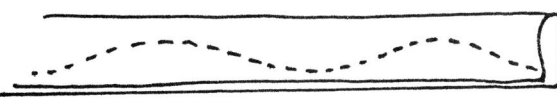

do it. Trim the seam allowances short and turn over a small enough Fasturn® to slide through the narrowest places. Drop these tubes on the garment fabric and they assume wonderful curvy shapes on their own. Pin at frequent intervals, then hand stitch in place from the fabric underside. This will take a little time, but why do you suppose the jacket this idea came from cost several thousand dollars?

Don't you just love to sew!

Many thanks to

Emma Graham
The Crowning Touch, Incorporated
2410 Glory C Road
Medford, Oregon 97501

Write there for many other ideas and patterns.

Program 8: See It, Sew It

Anything you see, you can sew. Go into ready-to-wear and gather up a bountiful harvest of terrific ideas. Try on some items you are considering to see what necklines are most flattering. What shoulder treatments best balance your hips and put you in acceptable proportion? Are jackets of a shorter length better on you than long jackets? Do straight slim skirts look better or would some fullness or flare soften? Which hem length does the most for you? Remember that everything looks lovely on the models gracing the pages of pattern books. Specifics are difficult to envision on your own body unless you actually try on the questionable item to analyze objectively. It is much easier to do this than to make it up and later regret it.

Jot down notes on your discoveries and be sure to quickly sketch some particular features you want to adapt. Not necessarily do you copy something line for line. Perhaps you just capture the essence of it and adapt the basic concept, flavoring it to your taste.

I had a very unusual fabric (who knows why we buy these things!!!) and couldn't imagine what I might do with it. It was a print cotton, basically black and white with red splotches at regular intervals. Kind of an Oriental aura about it, it was purchased for a sundress or summer fun dress. Looking through magazines and catalogs, I realized I was seeing the same little jacket reoccur in every designer's line. Suddenly this odd fabric started telling me it wanted to be that jacket ... but with some drastic changes made. Only selective parts of the fabric were used and the character of the fabric was altered considerably by quilting to beef it up to jacket weight.

Begin by finding a pattern similar in style to the one you are adapting. Cut it shorter or longer as the case may be, while you keep referring to the photo. Change the neckline or whatever other dissimilar features require your attention to match the photo.

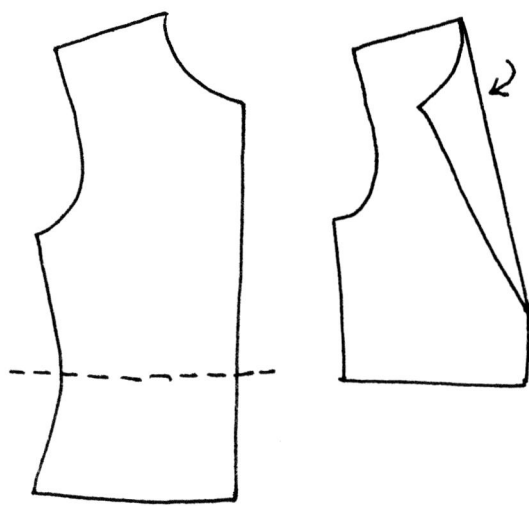

Move the pattern pieces around on your fabric until you find the best placement. This unusual fabric I used could look very awkward depending on the prominent design's location. The more unusual a fabric design and the more widely spaced are its primary motifs, the more care and though are required. Do not cut out too hastily.

Fabrics seem to take on a life of their own and dictate their terms if you work with them. It can be really exciting to see this phenomena develop! The final decision in this case was to use only the big red splotches for the main pattern pieces. All the black and white area surrounding them became the exterior facings finishing off all edges. Be careful when cutting one fabric layer at a time, as is necessary in cases like this, to turn each piece over to cut the second side. This will produce a left and a right.

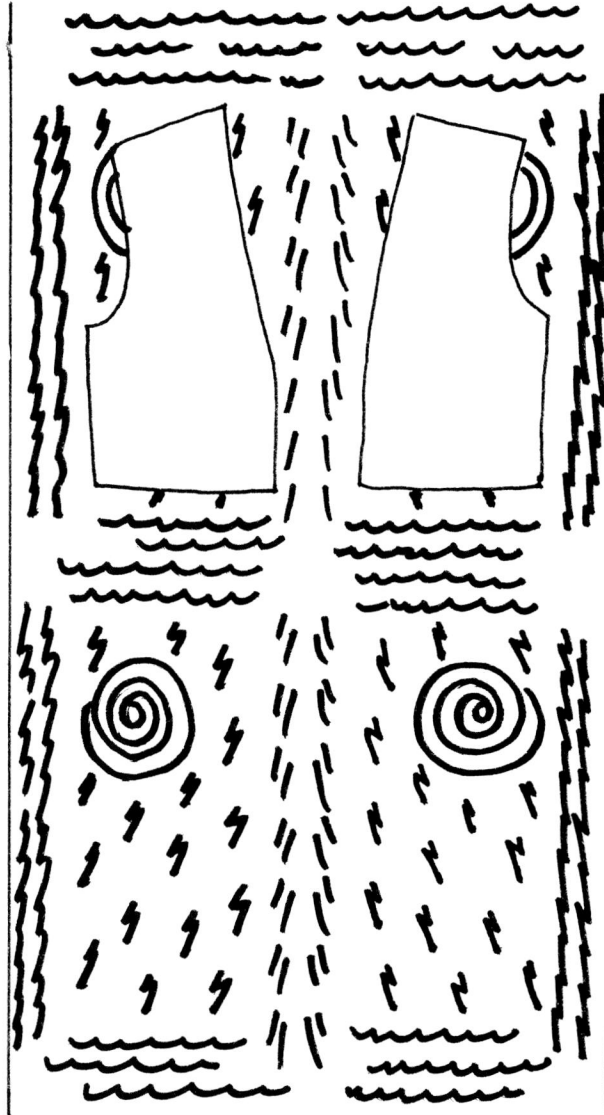

The next step is quilting. Spread out the lining layer on your cutting surface. In this instance white cotton was used. On top of this smooth out a thin layer of clothing fleece. This is not the firm type used for belts and bags or other craft projects. It is especially meant for clothing and is labeled as such in fabric or quilting shops. On the top, carefully lay all the cut out main fabric pieces, fronts, backs and sleeves. Carefully place these, right side up, so that each is on the straight grain. The fleece does not matter and could be used cut at any angle. The lining fabric on the bottom does matter, however, and must be on the same grain as the fashion fabric.

Use lots of pins all over each piece going through all layers to firmly hold them together. If basting is your preference, then secure all pieces with a hand basting thread instead.

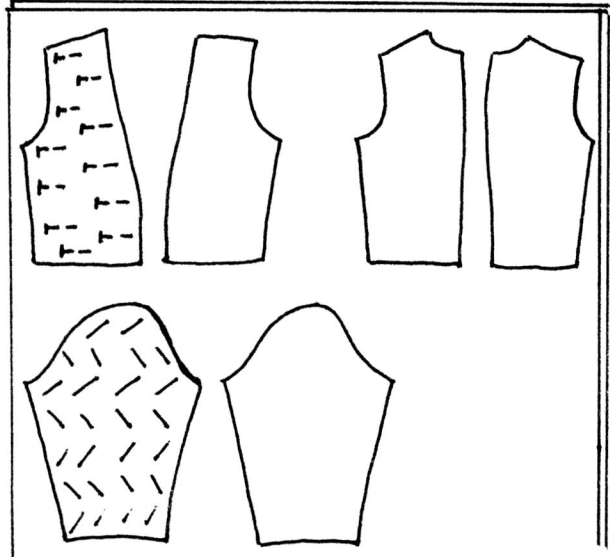

Cut around all edges and you are ready to machine quilt each piece already held together with pins or basting. The stitching design can be whatever you choose. My fabric indicated repeating the bold design, so the stitching began with the pinwheel. Then it just continued covering the whole piece with parallel lines gauged by the presser foot edge. Try a little of this on a scrap first to decide what foot will best do the job on your machine. It may be a duel feed foot or a roller foot or maybe just the general purpose foot ... whichever one you find you can use best. Decide also which thread will be the best color choice. The clear thread may be wise if many colors are in the fabric. A metallic thread would give a pretty sparkle to many fabric. For a summery

34

appeal, I used white thread which clearly showed all the lines.

For this jacket, the center back, shoulder, and side seams were then constructed. After machine stitching, one seam allowance of each seam was cut short. The remaining long seam was folded over it, edge turned under, and the fold whipped down by hand on the jacket inside.

An exterior facing can be applied at this point around the outer edge of neck, front and lower border. Because of the quilted jacket layers, this facing probably needs no interfacing. Construct shoulder and side seams so the facing pieces are joined in a continuous ring. Press the seams open and press 5/8" of the **inner** edge to the facing wrong side. Clip any inside corners in order to be able to do this. Pin the facing **right** side to the jacket **wrong** side and stitch the seam all around. Grade the seam allowances, turn the facing to the outside and press in place.

Now comes a fun finishing trim which is so popular everywhere. Decorative cording comes in all colors, stripes, metallics for colorful accents on harmonizing blends. Its composition is varied and any type can work quite well. If it is attached to a flat tape, insert that tape under the folded underfacing edge. Topstitch near the facing fold to secure trim and facing flat. This can be done most easily if you have a presser foot with a groove underneath which will easily hold the cord in place for uniformity.

The metallic cord I used was not attached to a tape so an alternative must be found. Those wonderful machines offer so many choices of stitches, changes of needle position, many feet to position the trim. Again, with scraps try the variables to see which combination works best. Illustrated is a wide braid foot through which the cord goes, so the foot precisely controls its position. Paired with that is a blind hem stitch which topstitches the exterior facing, zigzagging over to catch the cord every few stitches. The clear nylon thread should probably be used for this. Any job can be so easy if you let your machine work for you.

Buttonholes made vertically in the center of the band, buttons sewn on vertically centered in the other band, and the body of the jacket is finished.

The designer jacket I was copying had extended, tucked sleeve caps. To duplicate that on standard sleeves, simply cut the sleeve cap, as the dotted line shows, $5/8$" higher on top tapering to nothing at the notches. This will produce a little tuck 2" from shoulder seam, front and back, making the sleeves stand out.

When pinning the sleeve into the armscye, begin at the underarm and pin in smoothly up to the top 4". Pin the center top cap at the shoulder seam. The little excess on both front and back is then folded into a tuck and pinned in before stitching all around.

When varying from the pattern and doing your own thing, you must keep looking ahead to plan the proper order of procedure. The dilemma confronted in this case is that there will be a decorative faux vent formed by the exterior wrist facing. There is no way to topstitch this in place, even with a free arm machine, once the sleeve is in the round. The other half of the problem is that with the extra added to the cap plus the fact that this is a new pattern, never used before, the proper hem length is unknown.

Sometimes when plotting your own course, you arrive at a compromise plan. This sleeve seam has to be stitched under the arm in order to set it into the armscye. But it has to be open at the lower half to topstitch the trim in place once the length is determined. Half and half is the answer, stitching the sleeve seam above the elbow, leaving it open below. At the very top of that seam it also must be flat-felled by hand since another stitching line will cross it as it is set into the armscye.

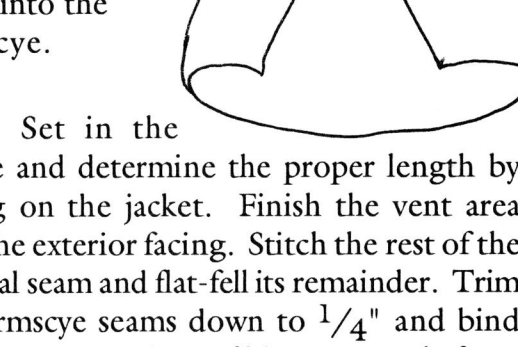

Set in the sleeve and determine the proper length by trying on the jacket. Finish the vent area and the exterior facing. Stitch the rest of the vertical seam and flat-fell its remainder. Trim the armscye seams down to $1/4$" and bind with a separate piece of bias tape made from the lining fabric to finish beautifully, as a very expensive designer jacket demands.

A little shaping in the shoulder area may also be needed. When a sleeve stands away from the jacket as this one does, a shoulder pad may not be enough. A little croissant padding out the sleeve may also be needed.

Cut a piece of the lining fabric as well as a layer of lofty quilt batting in an elliptical shape measuring about 4" x 8". Fold in half lengthwise enclosing the batting inside and serge the outer raw edges.

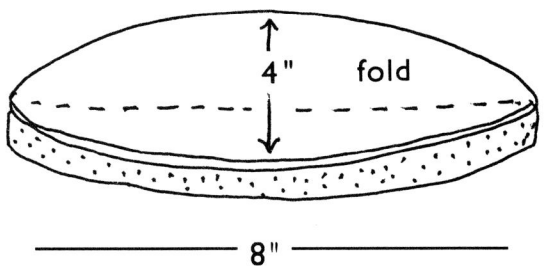

36

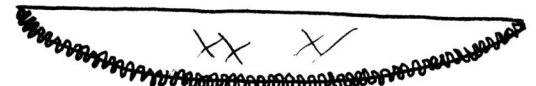

Hand tack this inside the sleeve cap or, neater still, enclose the serged edge within the bias binding of the armscye seam.

All this interior finishing can be eliminated if you choose to line the jacket instead. Designing as you change a basic pattern to your liking is a genuine challenge. It keeps your mind as nimble as your fingers and the resulting product is marvelous!

Program 9: See It Again ... New Flavor

Flipping through the fashion magazines and catalogs I keep seeing that same jacket, each time flavored in a different spice. There it is in velvet with satin appliques. It appears again in denim trimmed in UltraSuede®. Boiled wool with foldover braid shows up in another option. Audrey Hepburn wears it accepting a U.N.I.C.E.F. award and Barbara Walters interviews a celebrity in the same jacket. Fabrics, embellishments, finishes differ, but the possibilities utilizing the same little jacket pattern could go on to infinity. The price rage varies from $100 to up into the thousands of dollars depending on the fame of the label and the quality of materials and workmanship. Tear out all those marvelous photos you like. Pair them with fabrics you already have or can easily find in a fabric shop. Duplicate anything you see at a fraction of the price.

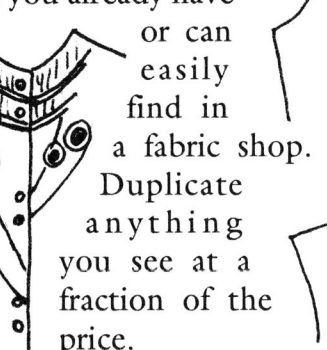

Isn't sewing wonderful?

The next jacket, same pattern, I chose to make was another wild fabric I found in my stash. This one was a linen print in bright primary colors with a liberal sprinkling of black mixed in. Over a black outfit to cool it down, this little jacket could be quite wearable. The variation on this jacket from the pattern I used was first a higher neckline.

This can be done by pinning a paper under the neckline area where you want it extended. Then line up a ruler on the shoulder line and extend that slanted line over at least to the jacket center front. Extend the center edge line up to intersect the shoulder line. Mark $3 \frac{1}{2}$" down from that point.

With a curve stick find a nice smooth curve to trace around completing the new jewel neck.

Trace this pattern (for a duplicate that can be cut up) $3 \frac{1}{2}$" on a fibrous pattern tracer or other paper. Using a hem gauge, draw a parallel curved line 3" down from the neckline. Draw a second parallel line another 3" down. Draw two hash marks across each of these new lines. This is because you will cut these pieces apart, add seams, and the hash marks will become notches to aid in stitching the pieces back together.

Pin this new pattern to a double layer of fusible interfacing of a weight suitable for the jacket fabric. Cut it out, then also cut on the two new curved line you created. With chalk or fabric marker, be sure you duplicate hash mark (notch) locations.

Repeat these steps on the jacket back pattern if you want the same neck trim to appear on your jacket back.

Now fuse the interfacing lower jacket pieces to the backside of the jacket fabric. Be very sure the center front line of the interfacing is on the straight grain of fabric before you fuse. Remember where the hash marks are, to cut ⁵⁄₈" seam allowances and make notches in the proper locations.

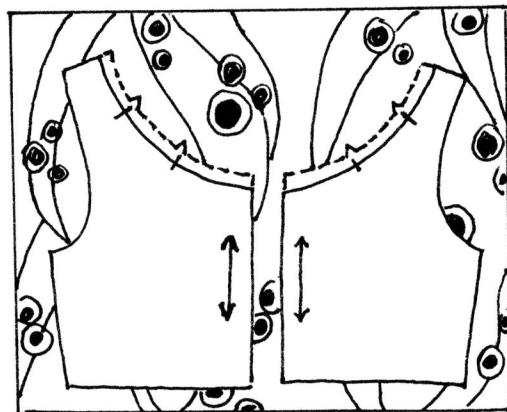

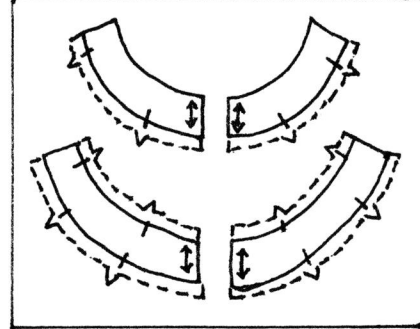

Repeat this on the contrasting fabric to be used for the neckline pieces. The upper neck piece will only need a lower seam allowance added. The lower neck piece will need both above and below seams added along with notches where hash marks are.

Use a commercial corded trim to accent curved seams where the pieces join. Or make your own by cutting 1 ½" wide strips of bias and folding it over two strands of yarn, wrong sides together.

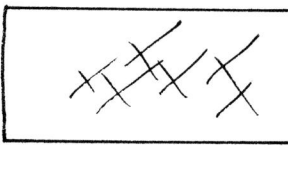

With the help of a cording foot or a zipper foot, stitch close to the yarn.

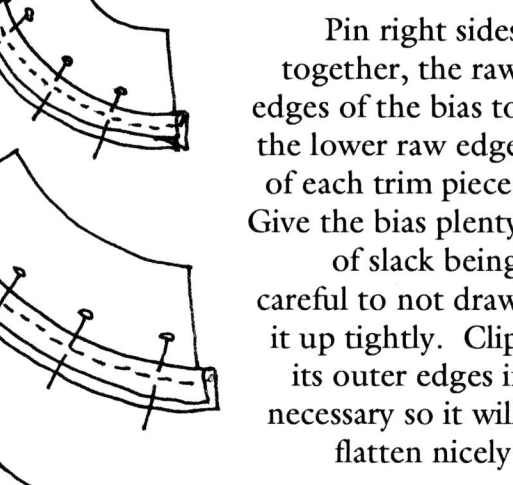

Pin right sides together, the raw edges of the bias to the lower raw edge of each trim piece. Give the bias plenty of slack being careful to not draw it up tightly. Clip its outer edges if necessary so it will flatten nicely.

Stitch, retracing the stitching line already made on the corded bias. To then connect the ⁵⁄₈" seams of all three pieces, it will be necessary to make ³⁄₈" clips in each of the **inside** curves as illustrated.

When stitched together, proceed with the rest of jacket construction.

Another jacket seen was our same little familiar pattern. A few pieces of padded fabric, cut in unusual shapes, appliqued on a shoulder with a satin stitch justified the big price tag!!! Aren't you glad you sew it yourself?

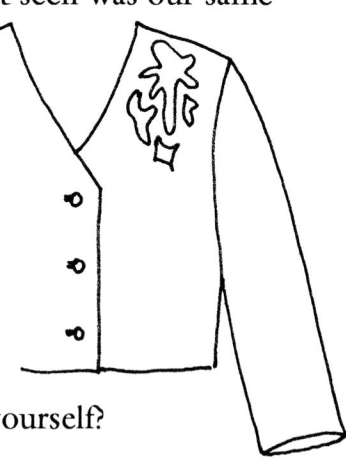

To cut out this second jacket, the only change seems to be a cut-on facing.

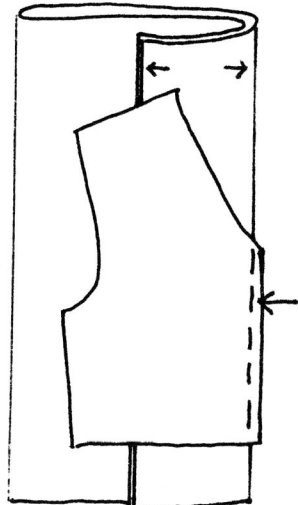

• stitching line of pattern on fold of fabric.

Fold the double layer of fabric back about 8". Place the stitching line of the bodice front on the new fabric fold. Cut out through all four layers in the front area, two at sides. Open up and trim down a little of the facing.

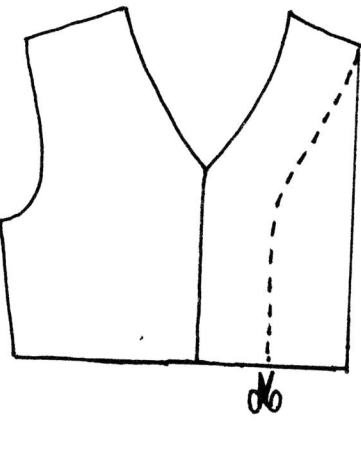

With very much wear, a woven fabric applique could begin to fray away from its satin stitch border. If it will be flat, fuse it to the jacket front first before satin stitching. But when padded and puffy, it may be good insurance to fuse a knit interfacing to the applique backside before proceeding since it can't be fused to the garment.

Draw a design on a piece of paper, cut a piece of fabric to be used for the applique (fused backing on it) a little larger. Place a piece of tear away stabilizer under the interfaced jacket front. On top of jacket, put a little fiberfill (quilt batting), then the reinforced applique fabric, and on top of it all, the paper design. Pin all layers together.

Straight stitch following the paper line drawing. Tear away all paper on top as its job has ended and it is no longer needed.

With little scissors (the pelican variety work well), cut away all excess applique fabric and fiberfill not needed.

With the stabilizer still underneath, satin stitch over the straight stitch line and the raw edge to complete. It looks exactly like the applique in the magazine and unbelievably easy.

Even some of the trims seen on expensive ready-to-wear are easily found in fabric shops. Anything can be copied ... or at least provide the influence to proceed on your own.

Program 10: Home Dec Camouflage

A friend of mine has a little problem in a home they just bought. From the master bedroom, a big archway goes into the bathroom - dressing room area and cathedral ceiling eliminate the possibility of a door. It can get drafty and a folding screen may come in handy! Maybe in your house a screen would nicely hide the computer corner ... or the sewing center. Or maybe with some fantastic fabric in its frame it would create a dramatic backdrop in a lackluster area.

The framework is easily found in catalogs or shops and typically has little dowel rods top and bottom to hold fabric taut in the three open panels.

If the fabric is heavy, it may be used as a straight flat panel in each, after finishing side edges and producing a top and bottom casing to hold the dowel rods. This would be especially appropriate for tapestries whose design is meant to be seen flat.

If only one side of the screen will ever be seen it is perhaps unnecessary to do anything to the reverse side. This means the fabric wrong side would be visible there ... should anyone care to look.

When thinner fabric is used, it is usually gathered up to two or three times the space width. This also needs only one layer of fabric as long as the screen will not be turned around.

The pink-blue screen photographed is reversible, opposite colors occurring on the backside. Since two layers of fabric have been used, either side is finished. Instead of yardage, two twin bed sheets were combined in this project. Sheets can be a good fabric source. The yardage equivalent is :

Twin	66" x 96"	or about	3 ½ yards
Full	81" x 96"	or about	4 ½
Queen	90" x 102"	or about	5 ½
King	108" x 102"	or about	6

These sheets just happened to perfectly match the room decor in color, but also the size was perfect. To gather up double fullness on the dowel rod, each of my panels needed to be 20" wide. A twin bed size was chosen

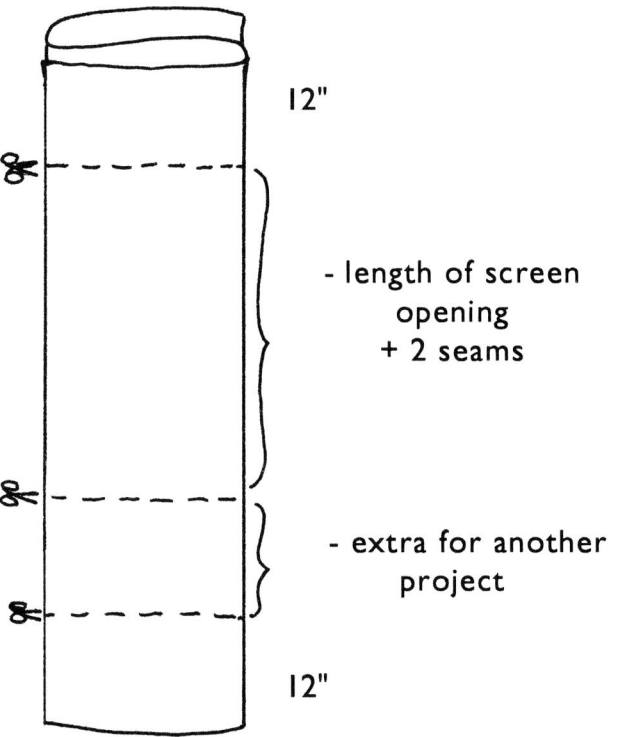

so that with the sheet folded in thirds lengthwise, each panel is 22" wide.

I cut off the top and bottom 12" of folded sheet first as they would be used for another project utilizing their hems already in place. From the midsection will come the screen panels, length of the openings plus two seam allowances. A mere seam top and bottom is sufficient because the screen panels will be double thickness. If a

41

single thickness will be used, add 2" top and bottom for foldover casings instead. All these crosswise cuts still leave a little more length for a possible third project!

Cut both sheets in the same manner crosswise. Then make vertical cuts on the folds of the screen panels as well as the top and bottom 12" pieces. Leave the extra piece remaining uncut.

Screen Panels

stitch seam all the way across
stitch side seams to within 1 1/2" of top seam

leave one corner open 8"
stitch seam all the way across

For the reversible panels, pair one of each color, right sides together. Machine stitch or serge the four sides as indicated in the diagram. Turn right side out through the large opening. Work seams out to the edge and press.

One inch from top and bottom ends, stitch a casing line. For now the dowel rod will be inserted next to the stitching, away from the end, so a ruffle is produced top and bottom.

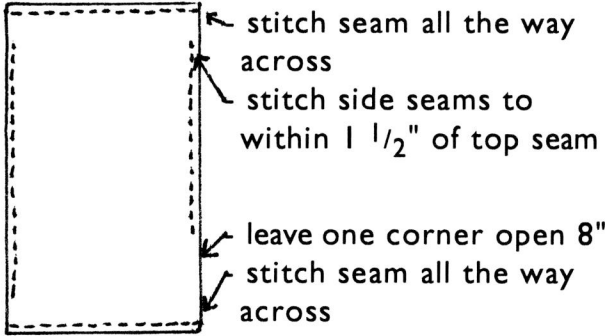

If after washing, there is shrinkage, you've built in the possibility of inserting one or both dowel rods in the end pockets, eliminating the ruffles. If a single fabric thickness is used for the panels, stitch a small double hem to the backside of each side. Press the top and bottom ends under 1/2" then again 1 1/2". Stitch two casing lines as shown.

Closet Shoulder Protectors

Your house has no dust, right? Should there be a little lint which lands on the shoulders of infrequently worn garments, however, a set of shoulder protectors to cover these garments might be very nice. The fabric covers permit the garment to breathe healthily which plastic covers do not. Also a highly sensitive nose finds plastic emits an objectionable odor in time.

Since these are made from the two hemmed ends of the sheet, both lower edges of the covers will be finished. In many cases the top hem will be decorated by lace, eyelet, machine embroidery, or piping. From the pieces cut, pair a top and bottom together.

To get the proper shape, lay a clothes hanger on top and chalk the slanted shoulder line resulting.

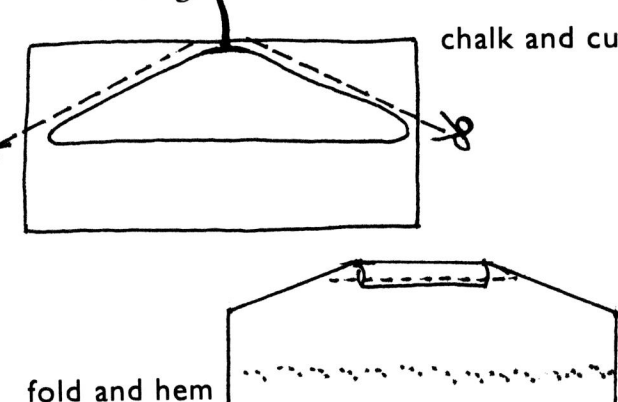

chalk and cut

fold and hem

42

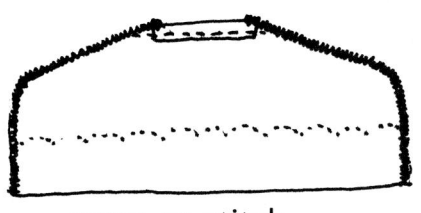 

serge or stitch

After cutting, each single layer needs to be folded down twice at the top center to the wrong side. That flat center should be about 2" wide. Machine stitch to hem the little area. It will later be the opening through which the hanger hook fits.

Pair these using a sheet top and a sheet bottom for each. This is so that each protector will have one decorative wide hem on the front side and a narrower hemmed sheet bottom on the back side. Right sides together, serge or stitch the shoulder seams. Turn right side out, press.

These make a nice hostess gift. Once you have visited in someone's home and know the guest room colors, these would be much appreciated as a thank you.

Lampshade or Wastebasket Slipcover

From the original sheets a left over, uncut piece is just deep enough to make a slip cover for a lampshade or wastebasket. This project will have a top and bottom elastic attached.

For a little exercise in self-discipline while doing this process, since you're already set up for it, remember the swimsuit whose elastic needs replacing. Sewing new things is fun. Intermingling the repair projects with something new make them seem less tedious.

If this slipcover is done by machine with an elastic casing top and bottom, cut the fabric height about 3" taller than the shade it will cover. Stitch a vertical seam to make the fabric a cylinder. The circumference should be twice or more the distance around the shade. The top and bottom edges are then pressed twice to the backside. The width of this turn under should be slightly wider than the narrow elastic to be used.

Topstitch the hem edges in place. Cut the elastic pieces so they can be pulled over the shade, but small enough that they tightly pull the top and bottom into the interior shade space. If it is a drum shade, both elastic pieces are cut the same size. If it is flared, the process is the same, but the top elastic is smaller, gathering up the slipcover more.

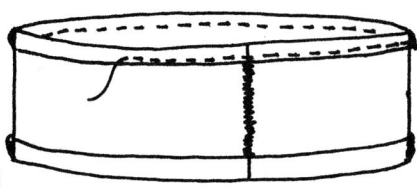

Another possibility for the lampshade is to use the serger which attaches the elastic and cuts off excess fabric all at once. This can be done with the general purpose foot, taking great care to not cut into the elastic sides. The elastic is stretched while applying. To be sure the measurements work out and the gathering is evenly distributed, first cut the elastic the proper size. Join its ends into a circle. Pin the quarter points of the small elastic to the quarter points of the larger fabric. Stretch as you stitch so that gathers are evenly spaced and be sure to REMOVE pins just before you reach them, as they would damage the serger to stitch through them.

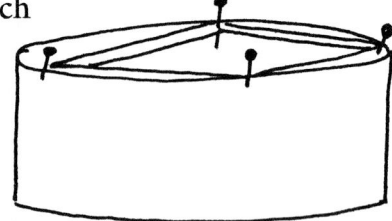

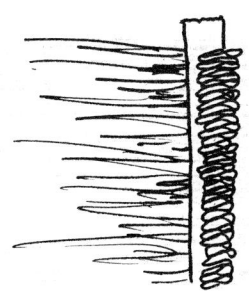
The same technique would work attaching the elastic edge with machine zigzagging.

On the serger, if you have the special foot that stretches out the elastic uniformly while it applies to the fabric, the job is even easier. To accomplish this, pre-figure how much the gathering ratio is by applying some to a small sample and adjusting accordingly.

Occasional Table

Another camouflage for the person with a small apartment, not enough storage space. Pack seldom-used items in a sturdy packing box. Find one the right size that could serve as a bedside table, an end table next to a sofa, or other occasional table. Measure its sides and top to determine how large a square must be cut for a cloth cover. Cut the square then slightly larger to allow a shallow hem. Place the fabric over the 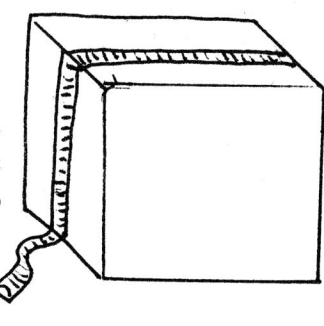 "table" and where each corner hangs down longer, trim it to the size of the sides. Trim this bottom hem with the various braids and fringes found in the fabric trim department for a fully decorated look. Or choose a harmonizing fabric from which to cut wide bias strips. Experiment on a scrap to decide how wide.

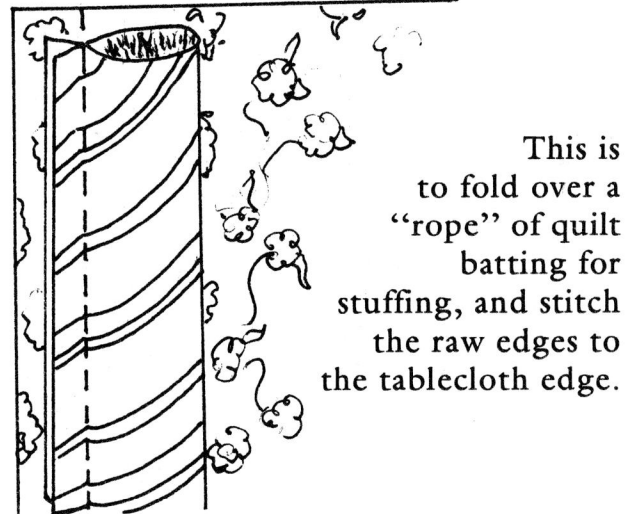
This is to fold over a "rope" of quilt batting for stuffing, and stitch the raw edges to the tablecloth edge.

Perhaps cut a smaller round cloth of a different fabric to put over the table top. This can nicely provide an interesting object which uses coordinates of the room fabrics. At the same time, it camouflages your storage box while furnishing an extra piece of furniture.

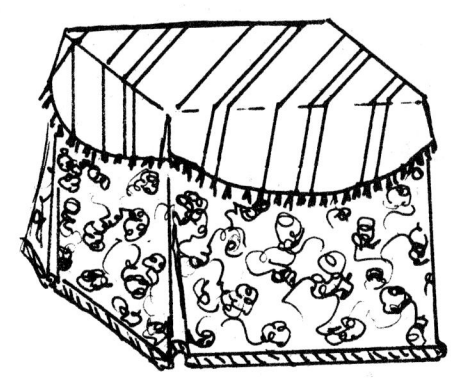

Program 11: Wearing Home Dec Fabrics

A walk through the home fabrics department will convince you those fabrics are not only meant for the home. They're also just great to make into big or little fashions to wear. It's a quick shopping spree because all the coordinates are usually arranged together.

The tapestries, cotton brocades look like they belong in vests or jackets every bit as much as on furniture or at windows. Walk slowly and think of each piece you like in a different light. I fell in love with a piece of polished cotton which looked perfect for a sofa in my studio. They only had two yards on the roll ... the rest would have to be ordered. I bought that remnant thinking the colors go well in a couple of rooms in my home. So if not the couch, it would become pillows to blend in other places. Not until I got home did it tell me to forget the furniture ... it wanted to be a jacket instead!

A little tip, by the way, on deciding about home fabrics. I really love to drape and upholster and I therefore do it all myself rather than having it done. Sometimes I walk into a shop and it's love at first sight. I absolutely know that fabric is right and I'll immediately buy the main fabric quantity plus a yard or two of several other complimentary fabrics for accents in the same room. If I need to consider it more carefully before deciding and investing, a small swatch is difficult to judge when it gets home. It might be a good idea to get a half yard to live with at home for a few days to help make the decision. If you decide against it, it can probably become an interesting pillow or part of a garment later. That's a lot better than buying the big quantity and later regretting it!

Log Cabin Quilted Tabbard

One interesting fabric I saw was a little cotton floral stripe. Actually there were a whole lot of little stripes of coordinated prints in this one fabric. It quickly occurred to me that this was the perfect fabric to use in a little log cabin quilted tabbard to go over a child's dress. This is a "quilt-as-you-go" technique in that while piecing together the logs, they will be stitched directly unto a mounting fabric.

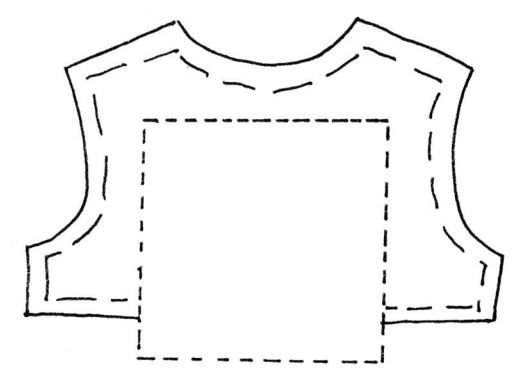

Make the mounting fabric square (back and front) of a suitable size for the dress bodice pattern.

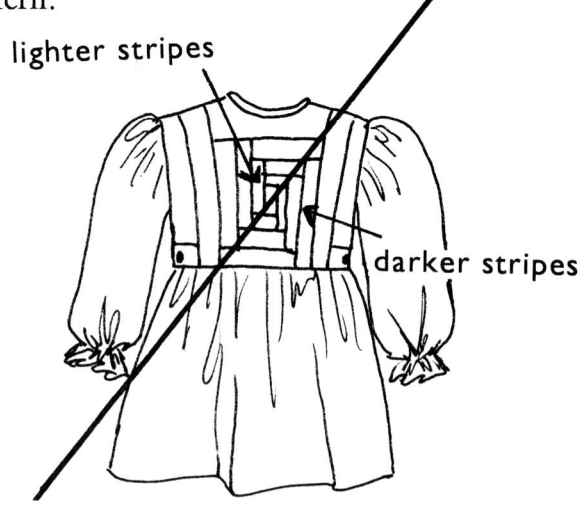

lighter stripes

darker stripes

Simply cut the stripes apart (some would have to be wasted to allow for 1/4" seams). Use all the lighter ones in the upper triangle, darker stripes in the lower triangle for the typical log cabin sunshine - shadow look.

Begin by placing the center square (1) directly in the mounting fabric center, possibly holding it in place with glue stick.

Right sides together, stitch a second strip (2) with a 1/4" seam. Trim off end of 2 and finger press it out straight.

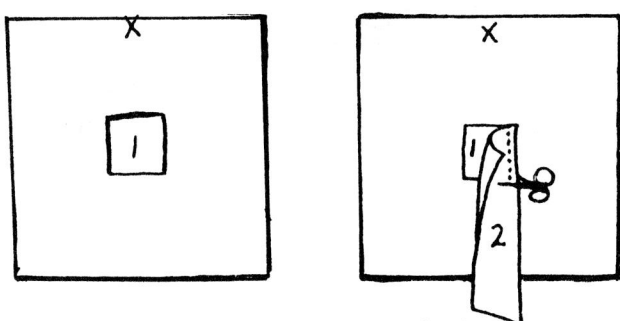

Turn unit counter-clockwise. Stitch strip 3 covering raw edges of 2 and 1. Trim end of 3, finger press flat.

Turn counter-clockwise, stitch strip 4 over raw edges of 3 and 1. Trim and press.

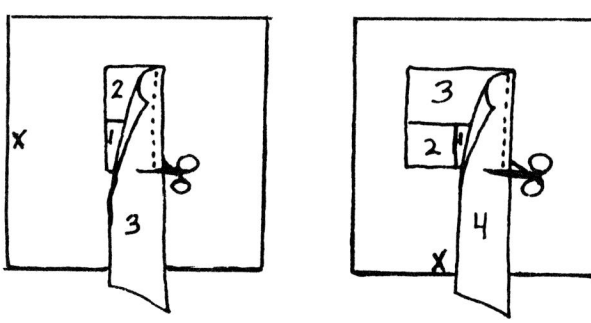

Turn. Stitch strip 5 over 4, 1, and 2.

Repeat this process until mounting blocks (make two, one each for back and front) are covered with the log cabin patchwork.

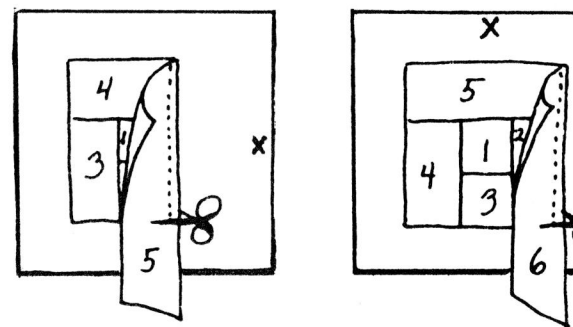

Finish edges top and bottom, possibly by lining with another fabric. Add shoulder straps and side-buttoned waistband. Or use this as the bib part to which a skirt or pants might be stitched to make a jumper.

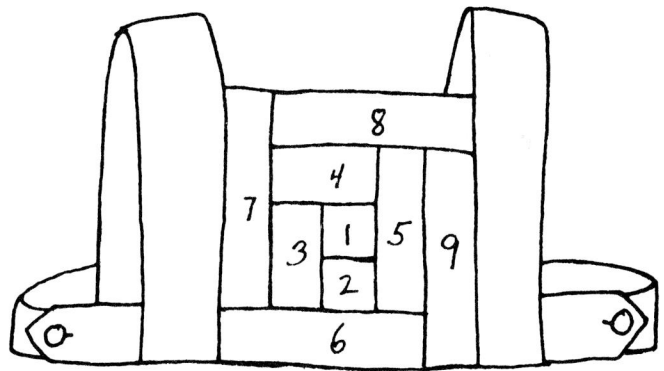

The sketch is slightly simplified as my little tabbard actually had 25 "logs" on each side.

Creative Patching or Embellishing

The clothes are going to wear out before small children do! If you're not ready to discard the garment, patch it with fun little pictures. Edibles from carrots to cookies, vehicles from outer space to under sea ... whatever interests your little one makes a good patch. These print fabrics abound with likely cutouts.

To temporarily hold the patch in place on the garment before stitching, use a little glue stick, or fuse in place by pressing with a fusible web.

Places which wear out first are usually located where padding might be a good idea, such as knees or pant seats. For this use a webbing of fiberfill $1/4$" to $1/2$" thick (quilt batting), a layer of fleece, or even a scrap of quilted fabric between the patch and garment. She or he will probably like the garment even better now than before!

Coordinating A Wardrobe

Whole groupings of coordinates are found in cottons which can make an entire mix and match wardrobe. Buy a yard, more or less, of several of these. I used a "Save The Earth" group from Springs Fabrics which coordinated in multi-directions and included all sorts of colors. Not only pretty, they could provide many ecology discussions with the child.

To get a head start on these clothes, I went to a discount store to find several sweatshirts, tee shirts in many of the solid colors found in the little prints. Then it's a couple of days of wonderful fun in your sewing room, creatively combining everything. Some examples follow:

• Arm bands on a sweatshirt need strips of fabric about 4" high and a little longer than sleeve measurement around. Press under a top and bottom seam, fit it around the sleeve to determine where underarm seam should be. Cut off excess, seam into a ring, slip in place on sleeve and topstitch edges.

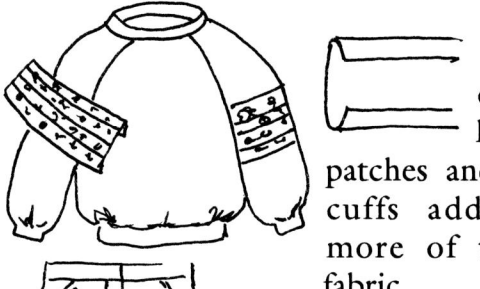

• A pair of jeans had knee patches and fold up cuffs added from more of the same fabric.

• A little jeans jacket with a stand up collar

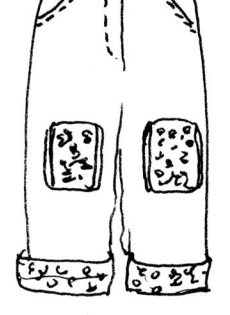

also had that fabric stitched on it as a casing, a drawstring (purely decorative) going through it. Word to the wise: at the center back, immediately put in a couple of stitches to hold the drawstring permanently in place or it will be pulled out quickly by the child!

• "Paper Bag" pants were made from another of the earth prints. A standard pant front and back pattern were overlapped at the side seam to save a little time by only having a left half and a right half of the pants rather than all separate pieces.

• Another fabric was underlapped a few inches at the waistline to provide a facing for the built-up waistline which will be added as the dotted line shows.

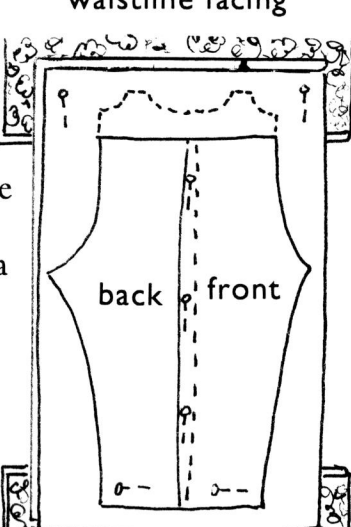

other fabric for waistline facing

other fabric for contrast fold-up cuffs

• Another fabric was underlapped at the ankles so that contrast roll-up cuffs could be cut out at the same time. Be a little efficient like this anytime you can!

• Another efficiency move is to mass produce two or three garments at once by stacking the fabrics and laying the pattern on top of it all. If your scissors won't go through all the layers, a rotary cutter will.

With long pants, or even skirts, children grow so quickly that grow pleats are a good idea. Just press in horizontal

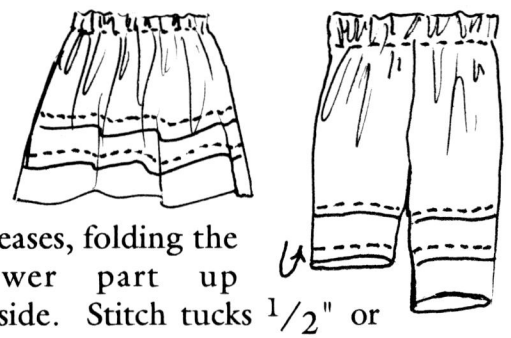

creases, folding the lower part up inside. Stitch tucks 1/2" or 1" each with large stitches to easily let out later by pulling out the thread.

• Those same paper bag pants then have the elastic-inside-gathered-fabric-tubes for suspenders as instructed in program 7. The waistline has the

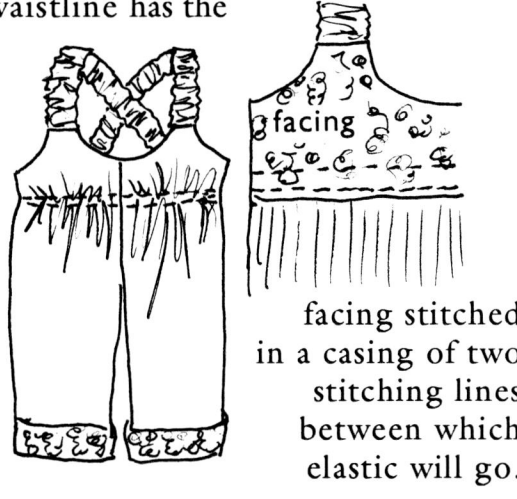

facing stitched in a casing of two stitching lines between which elastic will go.

Those ankles with their contrast fold up cuffs can be let down longer also as the child grows. You might then even use some slightly outgrown clothes. Enlarge them by cutting right through vertically to make them wider, horizontally to make longer, and adding strips of these print fabrics.

• With these pants, put a bright turtleneck shirt on which you've stitched several little patch pockets out of the pants fabric. If this is a gift, put a little surprise in each pocket to make it even more fun. Children delight in pockets so add lots of them (and be sure to check them all before putting in washer!). Put some of the pockets in odd places where they have no possible function. Children appreciate the joke.

• To one T-shirt, simply cut a 45" wide length of fabric as is needed for a skirt. Stitch a side seam of the selveges together, stitch a lower hem, gather the waistline up to the size of the tee shirt. Twin-needle topstitch the shirt over the gathered skirt top edge for a quick dress.

• Make a 3-tiered skirt of three different coordinating fabrics. For an adult, double the width on each lower tier. This might get too full on a little short skirt, so use some experimental discretion to see if it should be a little skimpier than this. The top tier is folded under to stitch a top casing for elastic. This is another skirt which could easily grow. Just add another tier at the bottom!

Think of the little jumpsuits, the swimsuits, and sundresses you could make. For that matter, think of the big ones you might like yourself. Those great cotton coordinates are every bit as appropriate for casual clothes for you. So do rethink the home dec fabrics and let them inspire you.

Many thanks to

    Springs Industries
    Retail and Specialty Fabrics Division
    104 West 40th Street
    New York, New York 10018

Program 12: A Baker's Dozen

I welcome the mail because of all the wonderful things viewers say. But too much mail comes to be able to answer all TV viewers' letters. I try to respond to some requests by lumping them together into categories and incorporating them into a program. Or in this case, using one outfit and the education it provides, here is a baker's dozen (or more) completely unrelated tips prompted by the three piece outfit in the program 12 photo.

The unlined print linen jacket to which these tips relate was actually a test pattern. It was being tested on a less expensive fabric to determine whether or not to make it of UltraSuede®. I was very thankful later because, although the designer pattern photo looked wonderful, the finished jacket had definite drawbacks. It may later be used with other fabric at some time, but definitely not in suede. Test patterns are terrific for decision makers. They provide the answers for whatever questions you have.

1. A glance at the shoulder slant when the pattern came out of the envelope was my first clue to a problem. Much too steep an angle, I immediately knew they must be more square and not only for my body. A glance at the envelope confirmed the fact that absent from the notions list was shoulder pads. This jacket really needed pads so the first change would be squaring up the shoulders to make room. $3/4$" was added to the shoulders of the back and front both for this purpose. Any time this is done, the sleeve must also have this additional height to accommodate the pad. The sleeve had a suspiciously flat cap. I should have known better, but I cut it out with only the $3/4$" addition, tapering to nothing at the notches.

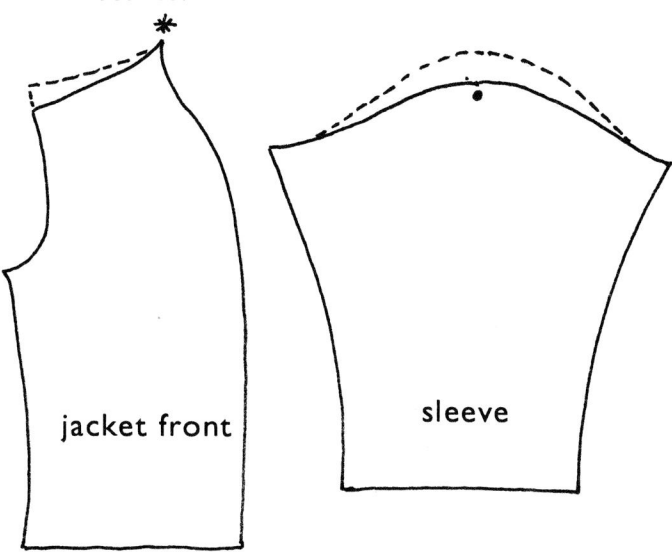

2. When these main pieces were cut out, stitched together and tried on, the neck point where there is an asterisk ✱, stood away from my body very awkwardly. One of three things must happen:

   i. Fatten up my neck about 4" to fill in the space;

   ii. Cut the shoulder seam as a straight line eliminating that curved peak at the neck or;

   iii. Build up the neck of the jacket to fit more flatteringly close. The back pattern neckline would also need a buildup to comply.

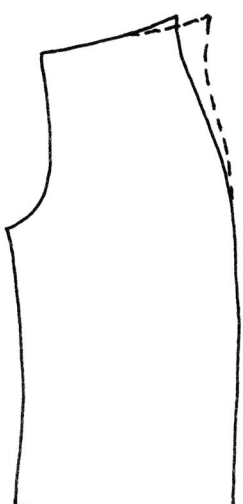

The number *i* solution, changing my body, was immediately dismissed.

The number *iii* solution could be done another time, but this piece of fabric was already cut out, so only the *ii* solution would be feasible in this case. Front and back facings would of course also need that slight change.

3. A sleeve should be perfectly smooth, free of wrinkles when the arm is relaxed, hand slightly out from your body. These sleeves had deep diagonal wrinkles. Wrinkles usually point to the source of the problem as these definitely do. My suspicions about the flat sleeve cap before it was cut out were confirmed. IF this pattern is ever again used, an additional inch or more is needed in height at the center of the cap. Do not assume that a more expensive price and a designer name guarantee a good pattern!

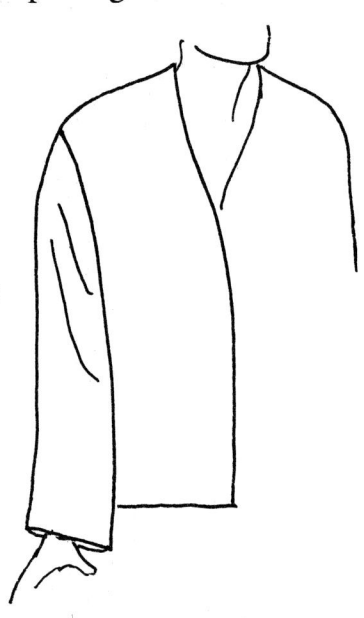

4. Slippery fabrics make it easy to put on, take off, and move around in a jacket. This is one of the big reasons for lining. Because the textural linen-like fabric used in this casual washable jacket catches, movement is slightly restricted. Lining would make it nicer.

5. Shoulder pads may be made removeable. If a lining had been used the pads would be between the outer layer and the lining and permanently affixed. The tee top this jacket would be worn over definitely needs shoulder pads (until fashion decrees them dead and buried). Because pad buildup would make this jacket look even worse, removable pads are a good idea. A 4" strip of Velcro® is cut, the soft side stitched to the jacket shoulder seams. The hook side of the Velcro® is stitched to the upper covering of shoulder pad. **Do not use the** variety that has a sticky backing as this causes skipped stitches and a gummed up needle when trying to stitch it on. Plain Velcro® machine stitches very easily. This fabric cover is bias cut as is the under layer, pad inserted between them. Smooth the fabrics in place, pin where necessary, and stitch the perimeter by machine or serger being sure to REMOVE THE PINS before coming to them.

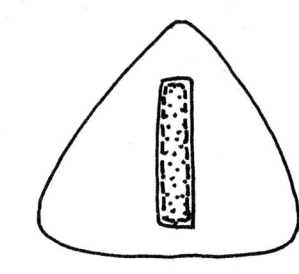

6. A lined jacket benefits by the extra firmness of a completely interfaced front as well as under the arms to support the sleeves and across the back shoulders for better balance. This is not attractive when no lining is used so the amount must be limited to within facings and hems. It is permissible to use a heavier interfacing in the neck and down front closures with a lighter weight variety in the hem.

7. If the front facings are held down with topstitching, it simulates a front band. This demands that buttonholes are made vertical to keep the buttons balanced in

the center of the band. If they are horizontal, they will slide over to buttonhole edge, off balance on band.

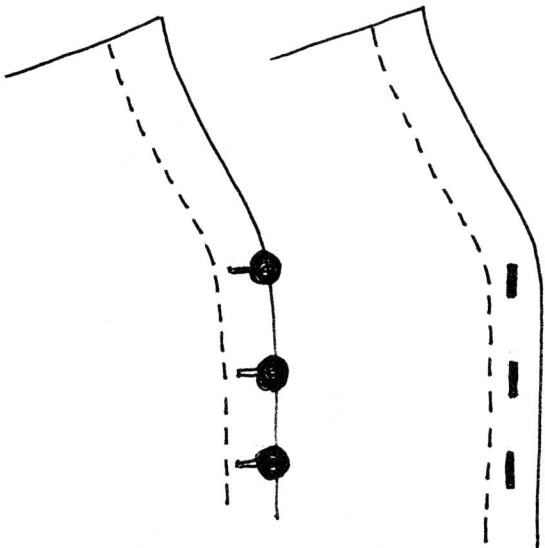

8. Buttons must be stitched on a garment in the same direction as the buttonhole. To contradict this would spread open the buttonhole unattractively. The shank length of the button must be the thickness of the fabric. A button reed or lift is useful in producing this when sewing on by machine.  If the button has a built in shank, you must sew it on by band, but its direction should still comply with the buttonhole.

9. To make a patch pocket perfectly blend into the fabric print of the jacket, first cut out the jacket and mark the intended pocket location. Cut a piece of wax paper the pocket pattern size, lay it in place on the jacket fabric, and trace the design with a sharp object which will make scratch lines in the wax. Locate this identical design in the uncut fabric and cut out using the wax paper pattern. A second one must be made for the other pocket to again trace the design.

10. If patch pockets look a little ungainly to you, try stitching their back edges into the side seam for a more sleek appearance.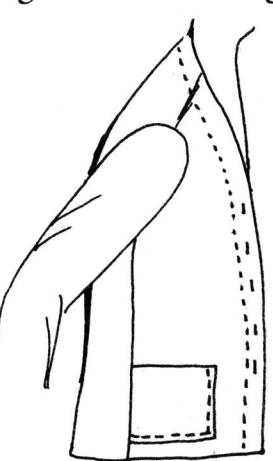

11. The sarong skirt utilized bias finishes at waistband and hem. Think through the purposes of such finishes and realize they need not be the same. The waist needed the bias both to neatly finish the raw edge as well as providing 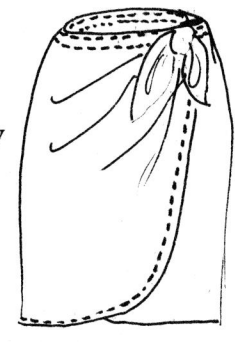 strength and bulk on which to stitch hooks and eyes. Cut this 2" wide and press it in half. Stitch its two raw edges to the skirt top edge, press out flat. Then

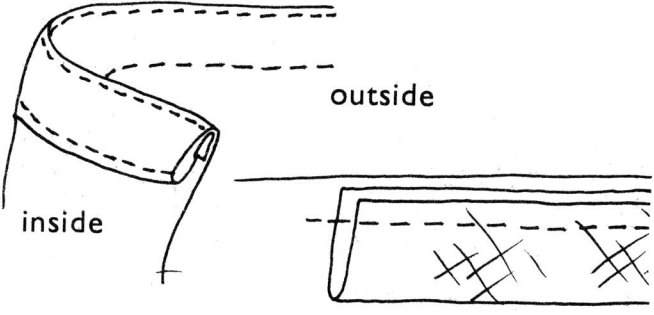

press to the back side and edge stitch it top and bottom for stability.

The hem only needs a neat finish for the curved edge, but wants no bulk. Cut it 1", use a $1/2$" bias tape maker to accurately press the $1/4$" edges to the

52

backside. This will curve beautifully around the shaped hem when stitched on, imposing little bulk.

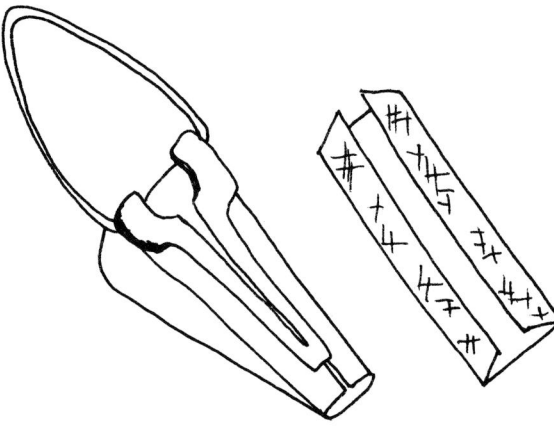

12. To hem a knit fabric, first serge the raw edge to finish. A differential feed can be adjusted so you haven't a stretched out ruffle when stitching across the fabric. Turn up and hem with a double machine stitch from a twin needle. Be sure to lessen the pressure on the presser foot so it won't force ruffles into the knit cross grain.

13. A tee shirt worn atop a woven print skirt can become a complete outfit by finishing the knit neckline with an exterior facing of the woven print. First cut a fusible interfacing about 1 1/2" wide, using the tee neckline as a pattern. Fuse to the woven fabric wrong side and cut around the edges. Press the outer 3/8" to the backside. Pin the RIGHT side of the facing to the WRONG side of the knit tee. Stitch, grade, clip, turn facing to outside, press in place.

Topstitch both edges of the facing. This will not pull over your head because the woven fabric has no stretch. Slash a line about 6 inches down the center front and see if it will pull over your head. A slightly deeper cut may be necessary. At the bottom, slash diagonally 1/2" both right and left.

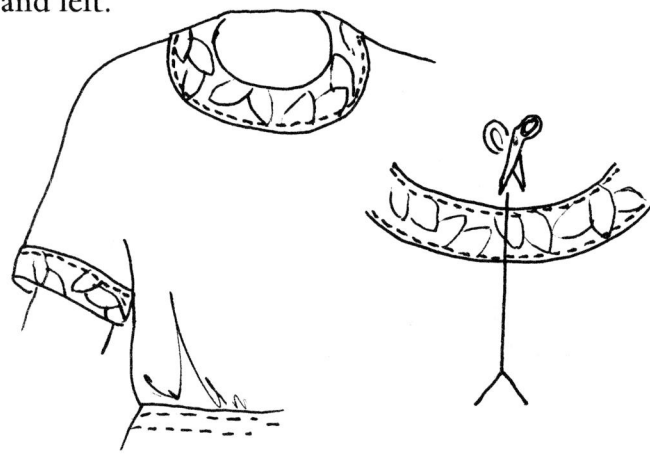

Cut vertical bands of the woven fabric 1" longer than the slashed area to include top and bottom seams. Cut the strips 3" wide including seams, for 1" wide finished bands. Remember they have to be twice as wide as the seam allowances because the edges of the slashed front just butt together. These bands will provide an overlap for buttonholes and an underlap for buttons.

Press under 1/2" seam allowance on each long interfaced edge (figure 1). Pin right side of **uninterfaced** band edge to wrong side of slashed opening (figure 2, page 54). Actually do the stitching with the tee side up so you can see where the slashed corners are. At those points, backstitch (figure 3, page 54).

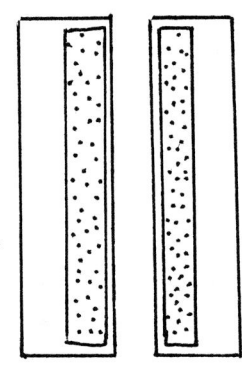

1

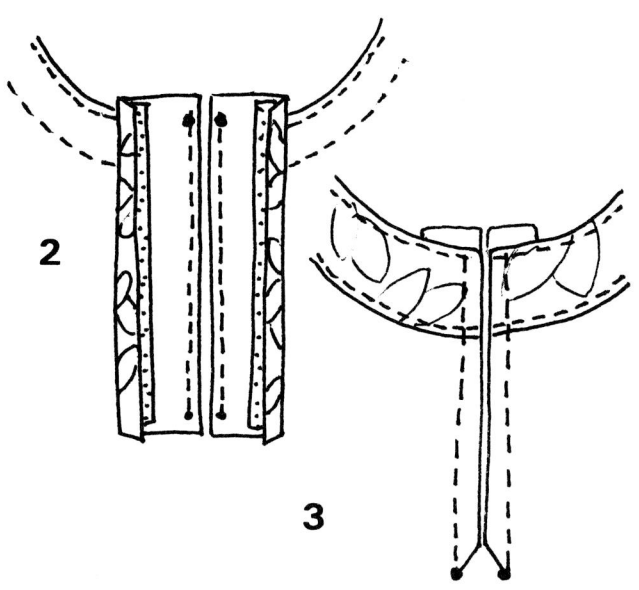

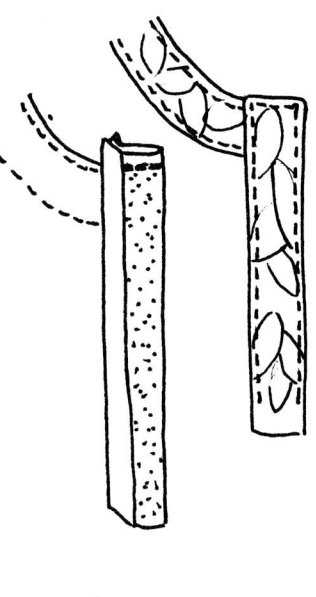

Press the band back against the seam just stitched. Then fold its top edge in half, right sides together. Stitch a top seam.

Turn this right side out after grading whichever seam allowances need to go to avoid bulk. Press. Topstitch both band edges to within 1/2" of bottom.

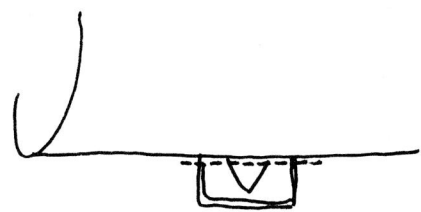

Tuck lower raw edges of band inside shirt. This automatically pushes the lower knit triangle down against the overlapped band ends. Fold the lower part of shirt up out of way in order to stitch the triangle to the band ends. Or there are a few other equally workable ways to finish up this band if you prefer alternatives.

These are just a few of the everyday solutions sewers confront in the completion of any project. Anytime you turn off a side path from a set pattern, you weigh decisions, make judgements ... part of the challenge of sewing!

Program 13: It's In The Bag

Recently we went to a wedding, a dressy affair requiring a small formal bag. Transferring all the absolute necessities from an everyday purse carried, a big problem becomes immediately obvious. That little purse will only hold a comb, lipstick and a Kleenex or two, as priorities are temporarily reclassified.

If I am going to design and create a bag, I'll start out first thinking space. How big does it need to be to hold all the objects I want to take along?

I stacked all my necessities on a piece of the fibrous pattern tracer which can be purchased by the yard in the interfacing department. Then gathering up the edges into a sort of hobo sack, I can estimate the approximate size the bag must be.

From that beginning ... size ... I move on to shape. This is all personal preference, but my favorite shape is a hobo bag, sort of crescent shaped, soft and squishy. It is easy to carry as it molds against your body, and its surface is a clean slate receptive to many design possibilities.

Thinking through how it will work, what pieces will be needed, the whole thing is first done in the fibrous pattern tracer. All the pieces are cut out and pinned together to make sure they fit, adjusted wherever necessary.

When it all works, make a prototype of any fabric at hand. This is a great way to combine fabrics new and old, and everyone can produce some terrific wearable art. Mix suedes and leathers with fabrics. Don't necessarily consider what's washable and what's dry cleanable. How many times do you wash or clean a bag?

You can also find commercial patterns for a bag, but here (next page, left) is the pattern for mine. The scale is each square equals 2", so the finished bag is close to 12" high and 16" long.

Fabrics needed:

- 1/2 yard fashion fabric   45"
- 3/4 yard heavy interfacing   20"
- 1/2 yard lining   45"
- 1 1/4 yard light interfacing   20"
- 1/4 yard fleece, fusible release sheet will be needed

Notions:

- 14" zipper,
- 7" zipper,
- thread
- gluestick
- UltraSuede® scraps

1 Square = 2 inches

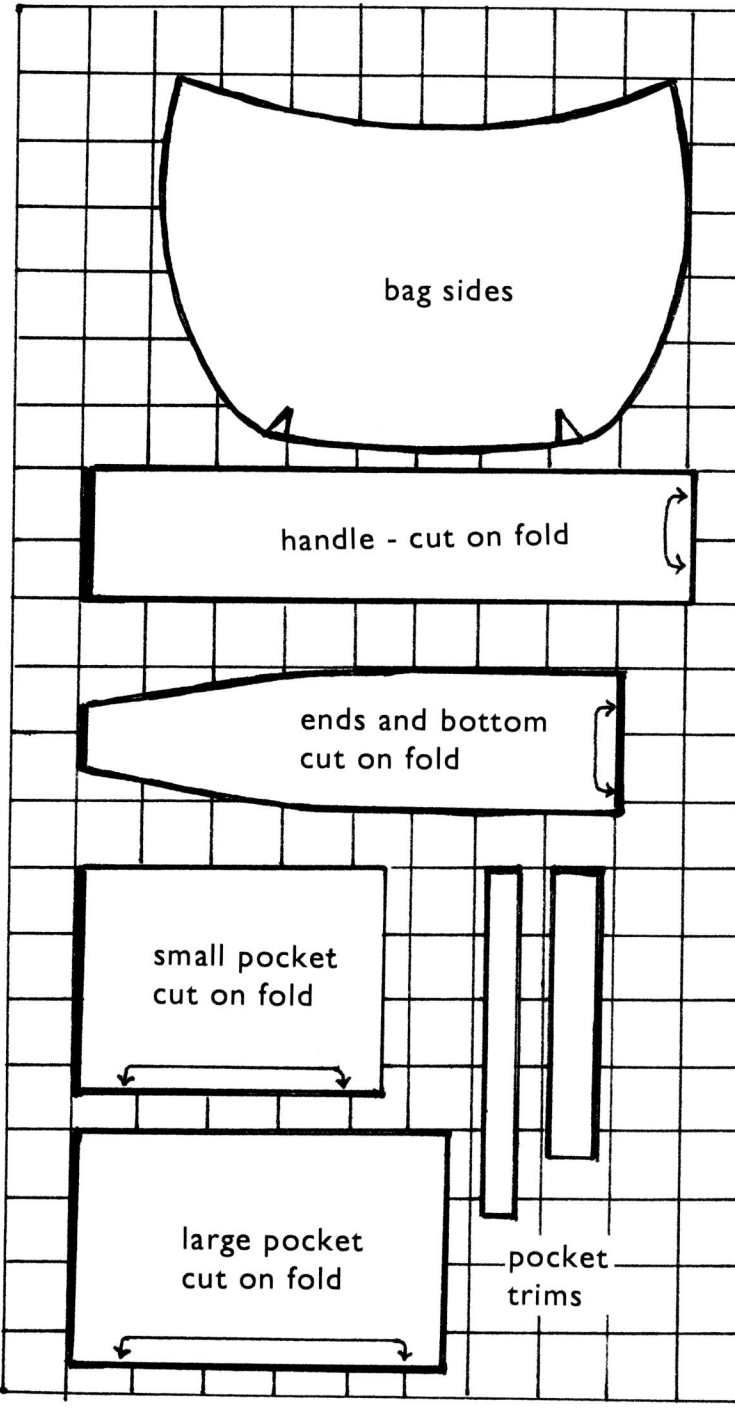

Cutting Instructions

Bag sides:
Cut 2 layers fashion fabric
2 layers heavy fusible interfacing
2 layers lining
2 layers light weight fusible interfacing (such as Fusi-Knit®)

Bottom and ends piece:
Cut 1 fashion fabric
1 fusible fleece
1 lining
1 interfacing (Fusi-Knit®)

Shoulder strap:
Cut 1 layer fashion fabric
1 fusible fleece with 1/4" trimmed off long sides

Small pocket:
Cut 1 layer lining
1 fusible interfacing (Fusi-Knit®)

Large pocket:
Cut 1 layer lining
1 fusible interfacing (Fusi-Knit®)

Small pocket trim:
1 layer UltraSuede®

Large pocket trim:
1 layer UltraSuede®

The fashion fabric can be UltraSuede®, UltraLeather®, upholstery fabrics, quilteds, or whatever you think appropriate. I interfaced each with a heavier fusible interfacing such as Weft®. If you wanted to beef it up still more, fleece could be fused to its backside. The bottom-ends strip needs the fleece fused to it for extra strength and heaviness.

The lining can be anything you like. In one I used a paisley acrylic challis left over from a blouse. Another has a rayon print whose colors were just right. Cotton print recycled from a throw-away garment lined a third. Any of these are strengthened by backing with fusible interfacing such as Fusi-Knit®.

The fleece used to beef up the bag bottom and shoulder strap is purchased by the yard in the interfacing department. This is the heavy, firm polyester fleece used in belts or crafts. If it is not fusible, back each piece with a fusible release sheet (such as Wonder Under®) so it will fuse to the fabric backside.

This is a relatively easy, certainly fun project. There are three units to construct separately, then put together: the outer shell, embellished in whatever creative ways you design, the lining with two attached pockets, and the shoulder strap.

<u>Outer Shell</u>: Cut out the fashion fabric layers and the interfacing for the sides. Fuse these layers, one to each back with press or iron using steam and a press cloth. Fuse the fleece layer to the bottom-ends strip. If any embellishing will be done, this is the time to do it, before the pieces are sewn together. Refer to the program 13 photos for some ideas. This is also the time to gather embellishment ideas from those seen in department stores or accessory shops. Magazines and catalogs furnish wonderful inspiration, easily adapted. The assortment of belts is included because these ideas are so easily transferred between the two accessories. If you don't like to wear belts, be creative with bags instead! In the bag photo the turquoise with its montage of UltraSuede®

scraps is completed. The burnt orange is just begun using an idea seen on an aqua belt. The orchid pearlized UltraLeather® borrows an idea from a lavender suede belt. Its outer shell is complete. The print lining behind it is also complete with its pockets and zipper, ready to be stitched to the outer shell.

As these illustrations show, after embellishing, pin the edges of the ends-bottom pieces to the sides and lower edges of the bag. Begin at the ends and work

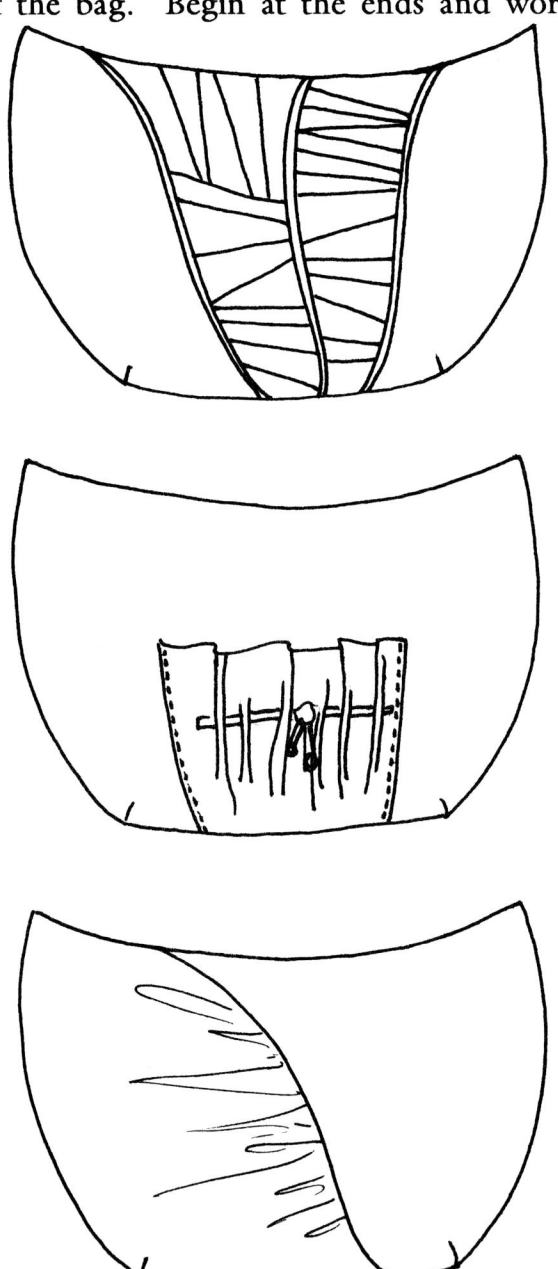

downward toward the lower dart area. Then pin together the center bottom and work out sideways to the same corner darts. All the excess fabric in the side gets folded over as the little corner tucks to fit into the strip. When machine stitching, leave about 1/2" open at the very ends. Repeat on the other side and the outer shell is finished.

In the short wider strip of suede, cut a slit 1/4" wide and 7" long with scissors or rotary cutter. Center it over the zipper, glue stick or pin in place. Stitch all around the zipper close to suede edge.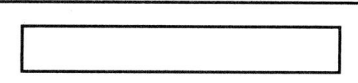
Center on the remaining lining wall and stitch all four edges in place

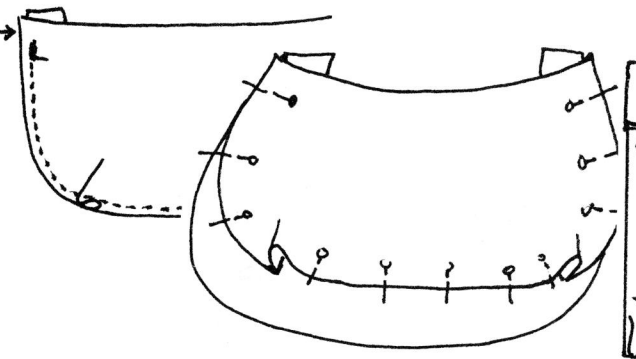

Lining: Back pieces with the fusible interfacing. Fold each pocket piece in half, right sides together. Stitch, turn right side out, press.

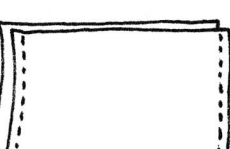

Bind the upper raw edges together on the larger one with the strip of suede or leather or even a bias tape. Stitch the remaining edges centering the pocket on a lining wall. This large pocket is like a compartment in the purse, large enough to keep several items separated from the rest.

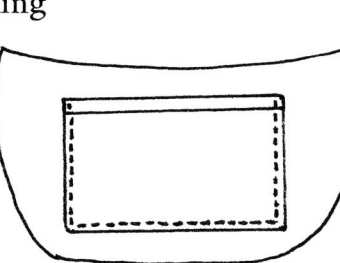

For the smaller pocket, lap the raw edges over the zipper tape and zigzag them to the zipper.

Stitch the 14" zipper to the two upper lining edges **wrong** side of zipper to **right** sides of lining. Use a regular foot as you will not be near the zipper coil. Position the zipper so that 1/4" of fabric extends beyond the zipper tape edge.

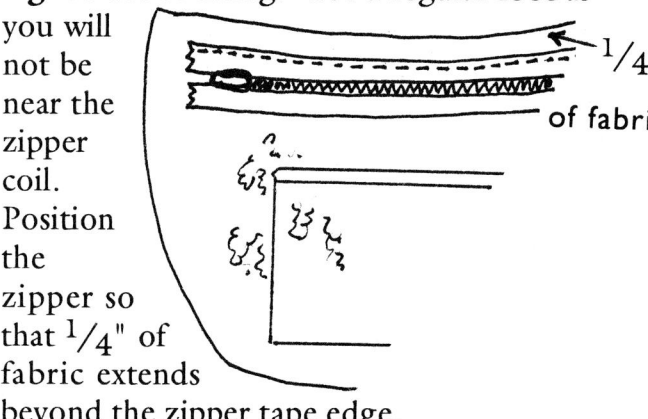

Repeat with other zipper tape edge on top of other lining wall.

Unzip the zipper. Pin right sides of lining layers together on center lining strip and complete the unit same as the outer shell.

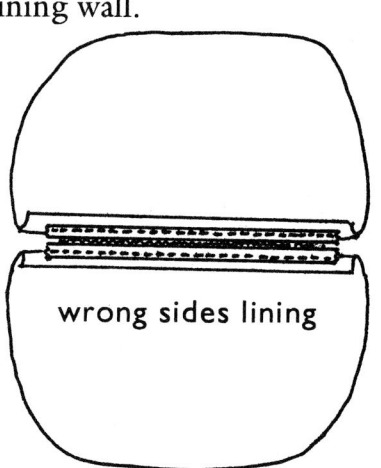

58

Strap: Fuse the fleece to the strap **wrong** side after trimming 1/4" from each fleece side. Fold strip **right** sides together. Stitch, then turn right side out. OR turn in edges, fold in half **wrong** sides together and top stitch both sides.

Put All Units Together: Stitch the strapends to the outer shell ends at 1/4" from end and again 1/2" from end.

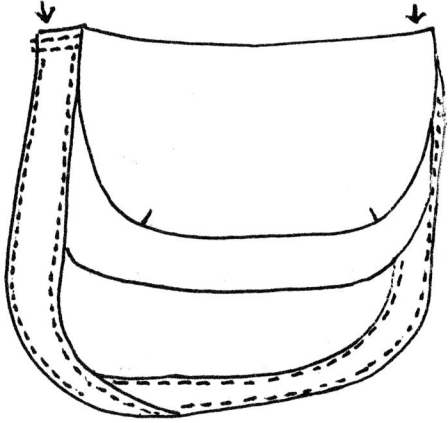

Insert the lining inside the bag outer shell, **wrong** sides together. Turn under a seam allowance of outer shell and pin it to zipper tape. The zipper (attached to lining) is of course **unzipped**. Stitch close to fold and again 1/4" away. The lining will not get stitched in the edge stitch line. It will, however, be stitched in the 1/4" line so be sure it is straight and flat underneath while pinning.

Repeat on the other shell-zipper edge. The bag-ends where the strap is attached are still open. Lift the strap up, the bag hanging below. This will automatically force the end seam allowances down into the opening. Fold under a little seam allowance on the open lining ends and with a hand stitch, whip the lining folded edge down to the strap inside.

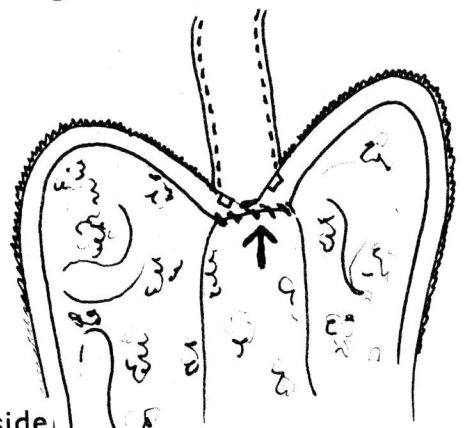

inside hand stitches

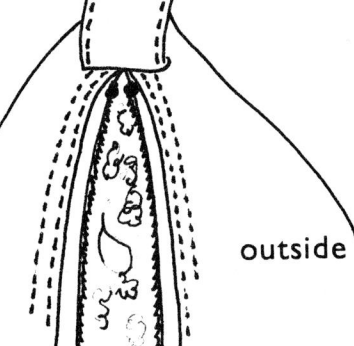

outside

If you enjoyed making this bag and would like full size patterns plus many design variations, write and tell me. I may do a whole book of bags as I have done two books of belts.

The joy of expressing ourselves, giving vent to our creative urges is a great reason to sew. This is the end of series 5 and I've barely begun on all I want to create and share. Write your public television station to express your interest in having these sewing programs aired. Come back to join me another time to keep connected to each other as well as to the world of fashion through our sewing. Until series 6, which is beginning to take shape in my mind ...

Enjoy!